Clarity of purpose and speaking up about what will make the difference in our communities and businesses is critical. Uncommon Candor inspires us to keep giving the gift of straight talk – for ourselves and others.

—MARIO MORINO, author of *Leap of Reason* and founder, Venture Philanthropy Partners

Nancy Eberhardt lives what she writes. She's honest in such a positive and constructive way that if she told you to go to hell, you'd thank her! The research on trust tells us that candor and honesty are at the very bedrock of all relationships. Nancy explains candor and the hope for building a culture around it. She provides great insights coupled with clear, straightforward language.

—STEVE GLADIS, author of *The Trusted Leader*

UNCOMMON CANDOR

UNCOMMON CANDOR

A LEADER'S GUIDE TO STRAIGHT TALK

NANCY K. EBERHARDT

Published by Advantage, Charleston, South Carolina.
Member of Advantage Media Group.

ADVANTAGE is a registered trademark and the Advantage colophon is a trademark of Advantage Media Group, Inc.

Printed in the United States of America.

ISBN: 978-1-59932-481-4
LCCN: 2014937065

This publication is designed to provide accurate and authoritative information in regard to the subject matter covered. It is sold with the understanding that the publisher is not engaged in rendering legal, accounting, or other professional services. If legal advice or other expert assistance is required, the services of a competent professional person should be sought.

Book design by Amy Ropp.

Advantage Media Group is proud to be a part of the Tree Neutral® program. Tree Neutral offsets the number of trees consumed in the production and printing of this book by taking proactive steps such as planting trees in direct proportion to the number of trees used to print books. To learn more about Tree Neutral, please visit www.treeneutral.com. To learn more about Advantage's commitment to being a responsible steward of the environment, please visit www.advantagefamily.com/green

Advantage Media Group is a publisher of business, self-improvement, and professional development books and online learning. We help entrepreneurs, business leaders, and professionals share their Stories, Passion, and Knowledge to help others Learn & Grow. Do you have a manuscript or book idea that you would like us to consider for publishing? Please visit advantagefamily.com or call 1.866.775.1696.

DEDICATION:

To my father, Howard Kahn, and my friend Josh Freeman, who constantly raised the bar for candor – and everything else.

CONTENTS:

ACKNOWLEDGEMENTS:

This is my first rodeo and I am in awe and so appreciative of what it takes to produce a book. This text has crossed the finish line because Advantage Media Group brought me a writing methodology and an amazing professional partnership that this extrovert adores. Special thanks to Brooke White, my guide and guru, and Bob Sheasley, my editor, whose wisdom, intuition, curiosity, and heart are even more powerful than his unmatched technical skills.

I am immensely grateful to my writing coaches Sam Horn and Steve Gladis, authors themselves many times over, who never gave up on this lengthy journey with me.

Thanks to Ashley Bedford Weckback, friend and colleague in Pathwise, who somehow simultaneously stays behind me, ahead of me, and in lock-step with me on this Uncommon Candor ride. Her contributions have been immeasurable.

They are the tip of the iceberg.

Below the surface, the following have contributed mightily to my experiences and perspectives of life and business, and, therefore, to this book:

Karen Conrad, Sharon Smith, Terrie Spiro, Beth Hughes, Kandy Elliott, sister-in-law Linda Kahn, and cousins Eileen Mollen Tanoury and Cindy Wolloch, each of whom reminds me every day that sisters are made, not just born.

My twin in life, Norman Kahn, and my twin at work, Stan Maupin, deeper thinkers and better writers than I, who always give me welcomed straight talk about how to improve. Drats.

My dear friends LouEllen Blackwelder and Susan Quinn, who constantly drove me forward (and crazy) asking, "How's the book?"

Jeannie Shaughnessy, friend and first business partner, who gave me the courage and freedom to be an entrepreneur.

My clients, colleagues, teachers, students, and coaches who shared many lifetimes of learning. All who have answered my endless questions about their experience of candor (or lack thereof).

And my parents, Dorothy and Howard Kahn, who gave me the best childhood ever!

TOWARD A CULTURE OF CANDOR

*"All faults may be forgiven of him
who has perfect candor."*
—WALT WHITMAN

YOU MAY BE OLD ENOUGH to recall hearing President Richard Nixon assuring the country that he was speaking "in all candor." It was a common phrase that he used even as the nation was realizing, during the Watergate era, that his honesty left something to be desired. His assertion, "I am not a crook," was somehow not the perfect candor as described by Walt Whitman, the poet of the American spirit, in the quote at the top of this page.

I'm sure you can readily think of the names of many prominent prevaricators: Bill Clinton ("I did *not* have sexual relations with that woman"), Bernie Madoff ("That was a nightmare I lived with. I wish they caught me six years ago, eight years ago"), Martha Stewart ("I just want to focus on my salad"). Some of those names that made the news are no doubt decent people who went through a bad patch. Others seem thoroughly reprehensible.

Candor is simple sincerity and honesty. When it lapses in a big way, our respect for leadership erodes. The examples are many, but the point is this: You can be sure that these celebrated cases represent a shortcoming that is deeply ingrained in our lives.

In boardrooms and families across the country, it is time to be open and direct and to communicate respectfully with all. Candor is a commodity of uncommon value to our society, and yet we see not nearly enough of it. In more ways than one, we are a people of uncommon candor.

> *Candor is a commodity of uncommon value to our society, and yet we see not nearly enough of it.*

We have so much to gain by remedying that. Research shows a significant return on investment from a culture of candor, a powerful tool that builds trust and is a force for positive change. Authentic conversation, quickly getting to the heart of what matters, translates into organizational success.

THE ART OF HONESTY

There are times when we communicate with candor, and times when we do not. The goal is to be more candid more of the time. It's within each of us to be totally lacking in candor at times, yet that doesn't mean we're unscrupulous. It means we are human. To be candid is an art, and we have to practice it to perfect it.

Each of us has the capacity to play so many different roles in life. The actress Meryl Streep has said that when she is acting, she is just bringing out those traits already within her that define the character. She is not faking the role; she *is* the role. We all have candor within us. What we need to do is bring it forward more frequently.

Like golf great Tiger Woods, we can practice candor even amid criticism of our failings. You may recall the controversy over an incident in the 2013 Masters. While some demanded Woods disqualify himself for violating a rule he should have known (but didn't intentionally break), others remind us that had it not been for two key factors, he would have continued the tournament unscathed.

> *The goal is to be more candid more of the time.*

A couple of at-home television viewers saw the ball-drop violation and called the rules committee to report it. Then, Woods himself admitted the act, without realizing he had made a mistake. He signed his scorecard and went on to deliver his media interviews, in which he said, "So I went back to where I played it from, but I went two yards farther back. I tried to take two yards off the shot of what I felt I hit. And that should land me short of the flag and not have it either hit the flag or skip over the back."

And there it was, a moment of candor about his approach to the game that became the proverbial nail in the coffin. He, unknowingly, admitted to committing the exact rules violation the TV viewers called in about. This, in turn, forced the rules committee to assess a two-stroke penalty on Woods. Yet Woods continued with openness and honesty, demonstrating further candor.

"I wasn't even really thinking," Woods said. "I was still a little ticked at what happened, and I was just trying to figure out, 'Okay, I need to take some yardage off this shot' . . . and evidently it was pretty obvious, I didn't drop in the right spot."

"Tiger was very forthright in his comments and his answers to questions that we had," Fred Ridley, the Masters competition committee chairman said in a press conference. "I told Tiger that in light of that information … he was going to have to be penalized."

Does Tiger regret his original off-the-cuff candid remark that, in the end, led to a two-stroke penalty? Maybe so. But, is it possible that his candor had greater, positive impact for his fellow golfers and for the institution of golf? His candor gave other competitors a legitimate shot at the title. Perhaps we (and Tiger) can see it this way: his candor preserved the integrity of golf by ensuring that rules are followed and players are held accountable by their honesty.

Candor might not feel good in the moment. However, it is this type of candor that allows an organization to be wholly more successful than its parts. I'm not suggesting we throw ourselves under the bus. I am saying that we have to foster environments in which honesty is such a habit, so welcomed, that we don't even consider hiding our individual shortcomings or mistakes.

Regarding his prospective disqualification or withdrawal, Woods said, "Under the rules of golf, I can play." So, rules are rules, including the ones that hold us accountable for our mistakes and the ones that work in our favor.

Many admire Woods, and some do not. Like all of us, he has flaws. But it's not as if some of us wear a halo of candor. It doesn't mean that anyone is better than anyone else because they are more candid. Sometimes we practice candor and sometimes we don't, but in those moments when we do, we tap into something powerful. Even when we are acclaimed as good at what we do, we make mistakes. If we think we don't, we're not being candid with ourselves.

IT'S NOT ABOUT OUTRIGHT LYING

When we're not being candid, I don't think we believe we're lying. When people want to point out an issue they have with somebody, they often will extol that person's strengths and then gloss over, at half the decibels, the area for improvement. That's not lying. But it's not candor, either. When you hold back or emphasize the wrong things, you lose your emphasis. It's little wonder that others just don't get it.

A lot of times when we're not being candid, it's not purposeful. It's almost accidental. We are trying to project something, maybe subconsciously, or we're trying to make a point, so we selectively choose information. On a first date, for example, people put their best foot forward. They project their ideal of themselves. If you have done that, does that make you a liar? Later, as a relationship develops, we find each other less than perfect. The projection wasn't quite accurate. And yet, in most cases, it's just the normal progression.

Similarly, people project their ideals of themselves in a job interview. Hoping to "win," many people try to demonstrate they have all the right stuff for the job. How much better if they focused on whether they were a good fit for the job. If you can't be yourself, you won't be happy, and a good place to start being candid is the job interview. Yes, it's good to dress smartly and display your best self, but trying to be something you are not cannot be your objective if you are to succeed. Yes, you may well adjust to the position and excel, but if you are making a career move, keep in mind that you likely will be happiest where the fit is best.

In the long run, we do well when we are very honest about our qualifications for a job as well as our interests. It's natural and desirable in an interview to want to make the most of your strengths and accomplishments, so long as you don't talk yourself into something you hate. A lack of candor can have such a consequence.

A friend of mine interviewed for a job with a financial regulatory agency, and she thought it was going well. She laid out her qualifications and background and references. Her interviewer, who was, at the time, a senior executive, thumbed through her resume and other papers and laid them on her desk.

"Would you like some feedback?" she asked.

"Yes," my friend said.

"I don't hear passion," she said.

The comment took my friend by surprise. She felt she had clearly shown she had what it took to do the job.

"I'm looking for someone who really wants this job," the executive explained.

At that very moment, my friend told me, she realized that the interviewer was correct. No amount of talk could cover for the fact that she just wasn't excited about the job. In fact, her presentation had revealed the truth that an astute interviewer could not miss.

In the end, the experience, though initially disappointing, was good for her. A candid observation had saved her from what potentially could have been unhappy and unproductive years. It also showed her the importance of demonstrating eagerness for a job.

Ask people whether they have ever had a "great" interview, yet never got a call back. Most people will nod knowingly. What went wrong? They imagine it was this, or that, or another thing, and the truth was yet something else, but nobody explains. My friend thinks the world of that person who didn't hire her. That frank rejection, she says, was a gift.

To tell the truth in kindness is a huge favor. To help people avoid the wrong path, or get on the right one, can save them years of frustration.

There's no reason to be offended if someone is being honest and tactful. To tell the truth in kindness is a huge favor. To help people avoid the wrong path, or get on the right one, can save them years of frustration. In the end, candor grows respect.

A TROUBLEMAKER IN RELATIONSHIPS

Lack of candor is the number-one reason for mischief in our relationships. Because of unproductive conversation, we fail to get the velocity and results that we desire. Our failure to be straightforward is a barrier not only to productivity but also to satisfaction. It's simply no fun to live under illusions, whether on the job or in the home.

We can make the biggest impact through straight talk. People want to know just what they are dealing with so that they can move forward. Otherwise, they can feel vulnerable or incompetent and stuck, and their fears rise to the fore. It is one thing, for example, to say, "Our public school system is not working." It would be quite another to say, "Teachers are bad." And yet without clear and straightforward talk, people might imagine the latter, even though nobody said that. Constructive communication provides a clear context so that others are less likely to take our words the wrong way.

We need to be open and direct, to speak simply and honestly, and to communicate respectfully. That hasn't commonly been the practice, and yet it is essential if we are to drive our organizations and society to higher levels.

THE ROI OF CANDOR

Among a sample of Fortune 500 companies where the CEO is judged to be open and uses clear language and shares information, the returns are well above the S&P 500.

As one might imagine, there is a return on investment (ROI) for candor, and it helps the bottom line. But you don't need to imagine. Among a sample of Fortune 500 companies where the CEO is judged to be open and uses clear language and shares information, the returns are well above the S&P 500. Among those where the CEO is perceived to use jargon or obfuscate, the results are lower than the S&P 500. That's according to data compiled by Rittenhouse Rankings, a firm that works with executives to improve company culture and leadership.

The firm ranks companies based on candor. In its CEO Candor Survey for 2012, it confirmed, "companies excelling in candor substantially outperform the market." It reported, "for the seventh consecutive year, the top-quartile companies in the Rittenhouse Rankings 2012 Candor and Corporate Culture Survey™ outperformed the S&P 500 Index of 17.9 percent, increasing an average of 34.2 percent." Although candor may seem like a subjective behavior, here it becomes quantifiable and the numbers don't lie. Points are awarded for "informative, relevant disclosure" and deducted for "jargon, confusing statements and clichés."

Rittenhouse Rankings has produced a valuable tool: The companies included in the survey have their communications evaluated for candor, and other businesses can see and learn how candor impacts success. Prospective employees and customers have an additional resource to make smart decisions about where they want to work or shop (or not).

Those findings should come as no surprise. Common sense tells you that when you treat people well—honestly and openly—the word will get around. More and more, I am hearing our global business leaders, top consultants, authors, and speakers make a case for candor. They are expecting it from themselves and demanding it from others. In his book *The Speed of Trust*, Stephen M. R. Covey opines on the power of trust as "the one thing that changes everything" and drives profits. Of his 13 principles, his number-one is "talk straight." To me, that underscores the importance of candor. Authentic conversation, quickly getting to the heart of what matters, translates into organizational success.

A SPORTING CHANCE

I love baseball. I've loved the sport since I was a girl, and Virginia has not one major league sports team. When we were kids, we would go to see the Tidewater Tides, which was a minor league team affiliated with the New York Mets (now the Norfolk Tides, a farm team of the Baltimore Orioles). What I love about baseball is the notion that I actually understand it. Baseball fans observe the whole field and get the impression that only one thing is happening at a time. If any game demonstrates candor, it's baseball, or so it seems.

When Tom Hanks' character shouts, "There's no crying in baseball!" in the movie *A League of Their Own* (about the All-American Girls' Baseball League in place during World War II), we are reminded that baseball is a sport of tough love.

Chad Harbach describes the game in his novel *The Art of Fielding*. One of his characters thinks of baseball as, "Homeric, not a scrum, but a series of isolated contests. Batter versus pitcher, fielder versus ball. You couldn't storm around snorting and slapping people . . . You stood and waited and tried to still your mind. When your moment came you had to be ready because if you [expletive] up, everyone would know whose fault it was. What other sport not only kept a stat as cruel as the error but posted it on the scoreboard for everyone to see?"

I know it's a complex and nuanced game, and I do love watching a game won purely by skill without aggression. I love that stadium atmosphere, all those people, excited and having fun, and it's all out in the open.

You see, athletes make mistakes all the time and their mishaps are splashed all over the media in replay after replay. But only in baseball is it so fundamental to how the sport is played and followed that error stats are as much a part of the game as catching a ball. In other sports, the stats tally the "positives": the touchdowns, the goals, the fastest time. In baseball, quantifying and recording a player's mistakes is an official part of the game. Those stats are recorded for history. Now, that's candor about performance.

Imagine if your boss were to keep a tally of everyone's successes and mishaps in the front lobby. To some, that would be embarrassing or cruel. But if the culture, the collective environment, is perfectly open and honest, mistakes aren't something to be covered up or forgotten. They are part of learning and growth. If we are uncomfortable talking about the errors, then we've closed the door on improvement and we've set a tone for perfection that becomes unat-

> *If we are uncomfortable talking about the errors, then we've closed the door on improvement and we've set a tone for perfection that becomes unattainable.*

tainable. Perhaps if every organization were as candid about errors as baseball, then we'd find more opportunity for collaboration and development.

I wonder if the players mind the scorecard's record of errors? My guess is that they're okay with it. They've chosen this sport and pursued it with a passion, knowing full well they will be identified by their errors just as they are with their hits, homers, and perfect games.

A TOUGH PILL TO SWALLOW

Johnson & Johnson's recall of Tylenol over 30 years ago remains one of the outstanding examples of being forthright in times of crisis.

In 1982, seven people died unexpectedly in the Chicago area within one week. It was discovered that the common thread among the deaths was that each victim had consumed Extra-Strength Tylenol. At the time, this medicine was the company's best-selling product and the top over-the-counter pain reliever on the market.

It was quickly determined that some containers of Tylenol had been tampered with after arriving on store shelves. Someone had placed cyanide into the tablets, many times a lethal dose.

James Burke, the company's CEO, had a decision to make. While it was believed the tampering had happened after the pills had left Johnson & Johnson's production and distribution channels, there was no way to know how many more bottles of Tylenol were carrying lethal tablets. Burke could have done what other organizations do at times like this in an effort to protect profits and reputation: deny culpability, say carefully crafted words developed to avoid litigation, blame others, and delay action. Another option, the one most focused on public safety and the more costly one to the company (certainly in the short term) was to recall the product.

Burke proved to be an example for all business leaders. He not only decided to recall the product in Chicago, but also extended the recall to all Tylenol on shelves nationwide.

Imagine standing in front of your management team and board of directors and recommending the recall of over $100 million of your leading product. Then, to restore the brand to a market-leading position, Johnson & Johnson would need to spend massive amounts of manufacturing and marketing dollars to replace the tablets and rebuild customer trust of, and loyalty to, Tylenol.

The Washington Post and other major news publications gave great credit to Johnson & Johnson, suggesting it effectively demonstrated how business ought to handle a disaster, using words such as "candid," "contrite," "compassionate," and "committed to solving the murders and protecting the public."

Not only did Johnson & Johnson give us a fine example of candor by an organization in the throes of crisis but, as part of the initiative to reintroduce a safe Tylenol product, the company also developed tamper-resistant packaging that is the norm today in the pharmaceutical and food industries. Due to these actions, it's likely that additional lives were spared. And within a year, Tylenol sales and Johnson & Johnson stock returned to precrisis levels.

Why do companies still struggle with acting candidly? What is it about the fear we feel in times of crisis that freezes us so that we act in a less-than-candid way? How can this example be a model that more organizations use in times of crisis?

Johnson & Johnson's leaders stayed true to the company's credo. They chose to do the right thing and were very straightforward. They quickly conceded that they didn't know where the problem lay, but within 24 hours determined that the poisoning did not happen at the factory or on the way to the stores. Still, they chose to be leaders. They communicated what they knew and did not know and what they would do to learn the truth, all the while emphasizing safety over profit. It was not an easy position to take, but it was the right one. Unfortunately, it is not hard to bring to mind examples of major corporations that have been far less candid in their approach to public relations in the wake of crises. Corporate leadership clearly has a long way to go.

In this book, you will find many stories about leaders who have learned from their experiences, and about my own evolution in learning the value of candor. Through these stories, I hope to illustrate the power of straightforward communication and what we miss when it is lacking. It's time that we create a culture of candor in our workplaces and in our lives.

CHAPTER 1

WHAT IS CANDOR?

> *"You must be the best version of yourself*
> *that you can be; stay within the framework*
> *of your own personality and be authentic.*
> *If you're faking it, you'll be found out."*
> **—BILL WALSH**

"I WANT TO TELL YOU," the optometrist told my father as they relaxed at the country club, "I watched you today, and I think you did a terrific job with the patients."

It was in the early 1950s, and my father had just graduated from optometry school in Pennsylvania. He was trying to decide where to start his practice. As he was taking the boards and waiting to hear whether he had passed, he was checking into various communities and visiting practices to find a good place where he and my mother could start a family.

One of his stops was in Lynchburg, Virginia. He walked into an optometrist's office there and saw that the waiting room was packed. He walked up to the receptionist, introduced himself, and said, "It looks like you're very busy, but I was hoping to have a few minutes with the doctor to see if I could understand a little bit about what it's like to be an optometrist in this community."

At that point, the doctor came out from a back room and said, "Did I hear you say that you graduated from optometry school?"

"Yes," said my father.

"Well, I'm swamped. I have an extra examining room, so take off your coat and pitch in."

They saw patients for the rest of the afternoon, and at about six o'clock, they saw that the waiting room finally was empty. "Do you have time to go for a drink?" the optometrist asked, and they headed out.

At the country club, the optometrist's gratitude for a job well done led my father to ask the question that had been on his mind, "It looks like you're very busy here. Do you think that another practice here in town could make it as well?"

The doctor took a long drag on his drink, leaned back, and said: "Young man, you are Jewish, aren't you?"

"Yes," my father answered.

"I thought so," the doctor said. "As much as I would like to see you locate here, this town is not ready to welcome you. I think it would be a mistake."

When I heard the story years later, as a teenager, I was furious. I said, "Weren't you really angry at him?" My father said, "No. It was a gift because I would not have known that any other way. While I may have been a very good optometrist, it might be a community where it would be harder for me to be successful, and I felt like it was very generous of him to tell me that."

The question had been this: "Are you Jewish?" The words were not, "We don't want Jews here." The doctor didn't say, "I don't like your religion." Yet we read things into what people say because of our experiences, our own biases, our backgrounds, and our fears. Maybe we get in our own way.

Certainly, it was a risky question for the optometrist to ask. My father never would have taken offense, but the optometrist didn't know that. He decided nonetheless that he was going to put it out there and trust that his observation would be helpful to my father. He was clear that he was only saying what he thought, and that my father, of course, could make his own choices.

"It was a piece of information that helped me make my decision," my father later explained simply to his angry daughter. And as I have further reflected on that story through the years, I admire my father for being able to accept those words and consider them a gift. He started his practice in Virginia Beach. "I think it was a great choice," he told me. "I could have ended up in Lynchburg. I could have decided to prove him wrong, but what good would that have done? It was just helpful for me to know that it might be harder there, and did I want to take that on?"

My father could have taken the stand, "I have the right to live here, and who is he to say whether I'll be successful?" Yes, one must confront prejudice, but we must be sure that is what we are dealing with. Sometimes the mere question raises the specter of discrimination. That's why you can't ask job applicants certain things, for example. And yet that optometrist likely only intended to communicate the prevailing sentiments of the community, not his own, that might influence my father's decision. They had worked hard together all day, and the optometrist deeply appreciated my father's helping hand. One could see that the question arose not from contempt but from concern.

> *Candor is honesty in communication that is helpfully forthright in a way that supports people's success and fully shares impressions of "how it is for you."*

People with hearts and with compassion realize when people have ill will toward them. They know when the candor is meant to be helpful. It can be a fine line, and it calls for sensitivity toward one another. My father was telling me that he was able to sense the motivation behind the words.

In any case, his decision to start his practice and his family in Virginia Beach influenced the course of my own life. Half the population there was military, and it was a much more diverse environment than most places in the South. I didn't recognize how diverse it was until I was an adult, but I know now that my opportunities were greater there. My father was thinking not only of himself but also of his family-to-be. He cared about my welfare even before I was born.

SHARING HOW IT IS FOR YOU, RESPECTFULLY

Candor is honesty in communication that is helpfully forthright in a way that supports people's success and fully shares impressions of "how it is for you." When someone asks for your opinion, and it's a sincere request, you are being invited to share your truth. It may not be the other person's truth, or the "true" truth, but it's an honor to be asked for your perspective.

As you respond, candor is crucial. Your challenge is to avoid belittling or judging or critiquing and simply state how it is for you. The short-term consequences might be uncomfortable at times, but you are forging a better future for the long term.

I think of the persona of Simon Cowell as a talent judge on the show *American Idol*. His abrasive approach to many of the contestants, even the ultimately successful ones, didn't seem motivated by a commitment to their success, even though such negativity might have prompted some to determination. Insults injure far more often than they inspire. At times, Cowell just seemed outrageous. There is a difference between candor and being obnoxiously blunt. To be candid is not to be insulting.

> *Your challenge is to avoid belittling or judging or critiquing and simply state how it is for you.*

I have a friend whose boss berated her after every presentation to clients. The words weren't supportive of her success. They were simply belittling, and over time, her confidence in presenting to others worsened. She lost self-esteem and felt cowed. The message was not one of "Let's work together for a better outcome."

That's the nature of candor. Instead, her boss was simply abusive.

Sometimes abusive people will rationalize what amounts to cruelty with words such as, "Oh, you've got to stop being so sensitive. This is for your own good." Parents can be that way. Spouses can be that way. We should communicate where we feel things need to improve. If people disappoint us or fall short of expectations, it's often good to let them know, but in a way that doesn't smash them flat.

Candor is respectful. It is committed to success. It is interested in a better outcome for all involved.

CANDOR AS A CURE

There is significant anecdotal evidence that explanations and apologies from medical personnel bring better patient, hospital, and financial outcomes. Many adopters and reviewers of "communication and resolution programs" report increased benefits, such as patient safety and satisfaction, reduced medical liability costs, and increased teamwork in hospitals.

> *Breakdowns in communication cause more hospital mishaps than equipment failure and inadequate training combined.*

Dr. Marty Makary, author of *Unaccountable: What Hospitals Won't Tell You and How Transparency Can Revolutionize Health Care* points out that "the Joint Commission, the accreditation organization for hospitals, reports that breakdowns in communication cause more hospital mishaps than equipment failure and inadequate training combined." He talks about the culture of not questioning doctors, the reluctance of those with less medical training to assert themselves, and he calls for a culture of speaking up.

In a 2012 article in *The Washington Post*, Kerry O'Connell tells how a fall off a ladder led to multiple surgeries for a dislocated elbow, paralysis, therapy, and a major infection.

As he dealt with his caregivers, he endured the kind of experience that can severely undermine trust in the medical system. Yet he spoke about one wonderful moment when a physician gave him straight talk. In the article, O'Connor talks about his ordeal:

> *It had been 11 months since I'd fallen off the ladder. Now I had a damaged elbow without its needed titanium implant, a paralyzed hand, and a forever numb foot. I was seriously considering asking for my arm to be cut off when my [second] surgeon walked in. He surprised me. "Kerry," he said, "I am so sorry for giving you this infection. I don't know how it happened."*
>
> *He said it humbly, with sincerity. It was an unforgettable act of courage on his part. It gave me the strength to not give up hope and to consider yet another trip to the operating room.*

The Massachusetts Medical Society is a leader in a program called "Disclosure, Apology, and Offer" in which physicians admit mistakes, make an apology, and offer to settle the issue. These programs are in stark contrast to the "deny and defend" strategy among some health professionals.

Is it worrisome that candor in the medical realm has gone so awry that it has had to be defined, officially stated, and described in recent initiatives and programs? Or is it refreshing that a profession with so much at risk has placed such great value in being forthright?

> *The Massachusetts Medical Society is a leader in a program called "Disclosure, Apology, and Offer" in which physicians admit mistakes, make an apology, and offer to settle the issue.*

A colleague of mine who was the executive director of a nonprofit told me about a time when he was having a biopsy for non-Hodgkin's lymphoma. He woke from surgery and alerted the nurse that he was unable to breathe whenever he lay back on the pillow. The nurse assured him it was a normal post-op reaction. Two hours later, he had a violent coughing fit and felt something at the back of his throat. He reached in and pulled out a four-by-four-inch piece of gauze.

The next day, a young doctor came in to talk with him about what had happened. The operating team had been using a medical device in his throat and at one point had inserted several gauze pads to stop a leak. This didn't work so they pulled everything out to start over but miscounted the pads. One was left in his windpipe, and as the procedure continued, it was pushed farther and farther down.

The young doctor seemed nervous, my colleague told me, but he was completely forthcoming. He provided every detail about what must have happened, and apologized profusely.

"I've often wondered how much that doctor was worried about getting sued," my colleague said. "But I was happy just knowing what had happened and being able to get a good night's sleep, and I appreciated his honesty. That was enough for me."

Later, he asked his oncologist if he had heard about the operating room incident. "I sure have," the doctor told him. "Your picture is on all four walls of that operating room, with one word written under it: 'Count!'"

SUCCINCT AND DIRECT TALK

Candor, by its nature, also is succinct, without irrelevant information. When we're uncertain or uncomfortable, we tend to use a lot of words. Sometimes people just won't stop talking long after they have made the point. The real message tends to get lost.

> *Candor, by its nature, also is succinct, without irrelevant information.*

All those words are the speaker's attempt to feel more comfortable. They're like a nervous attempt to fill up space in a conversation. They're not for the listener's benefit, and they blur the message. Some people can't abide the silence, yet sometimes, it's during silence that we become most thoughtful and reflective.

Similarly, when people are preparing to deliver news that feels uncomfortable, they tend to first try to build up the listener and confirm the relationship. They emphasize whatever they can find that might be good about a situation. Maybe they think they are helping the listener to feel comfortable, but mostly, they are helping themselves to feel comfortable, and in so doing, they are causing confusion. Sometimes people will soften the message somewhat, out of respect, but they should never do so to avoid discomfort.

If we are skirting the real issues, we are doing nothing to solve the problem. It's all right to feel uncomfortable. That's human. But it's a mistake when that discomfort leads us to start out like this: "You know, I really like a lot about what you do here." Those words should be reserved for opening a conversation about a promotion, not about probation.

Many people say that it feels patronizing when the bearer of bad news is full of compliments. When the real news comes—a warning, transfer, demotion, firing—the whole affair can seem less than sincere, maybe even weaselly. And that's because of the lack of clarity from the start. If there is really only one thing to say, then say it: "We have a serious problem here, and we need to deal with it, so this is what we are going to do, and this is what we require of you." That is a pure and honorable approach and a clear one.

> *The conversation becomes more of a partnership and less of a power show, and invariably feels more respectful.*

When you are short and to the point, it is up to your listener to ask for further clarification if he or she does not fully understand: "What do you mean by that?" or "Tell me more, I don't quite follow you." You have done your part in defining the core conversation and inviting the listener to inquire further. The conversation becomes more of a partnership and less of a power show, and invariably feels more respectful. The conversation feels open to both parties.

I once was a leader in a company that had to lay off a significant number of people. I was in a lot of those conversations. For about four months, we had seen that the layoffs were a possibility. In that time, we remained direct and open about the circumstances of the company. As a result, when we sat down with employees to lay them off, they told us it wasn't what they wanted to hear, but they had known it would be coming if the situation didn't turn around. They felt well treated, even when given the bad news. That was over a decade ago, and many of them maintained their relationships with the company.

One thing we did not tell employees was how hard it was for us. You can be sure that the person across the table, the one who really is getting the hard news, doesn't want to hear it. I suppose people who make such a comment are intending to communicate that they don't take this lightly, but it comes across as, "I care more about my pain than yours." It sounds particularly insincere from someone you know is making beaucoup bucks. Another less-than-appropriate line that people sometimes use in such situations is, "I want to be totally honest with you." Colleagues report that when they have heard that, they felt like asking, "So does that mean you haven't been honest all along?"

We must be careful with our words. Particularly in times of crisis and of high emotion, they can be taken the wrong way if used carelessly. People will sense right away if we aren't being genuine. And when we are being genuine, it will show.

WHY CANDOR MATTERS

When someone honors us by asking for our opinion, it is best, in our response, if we trim away what is irrelevant and address what really matters. A lot of excess verbiage is unproductive and can actually be confusing.

We should cut through to the nuggets of a conversation. Sometimes, when people ask for an opinion, a part of them doesn't want to know the truth. But if they ask you, deliver your opinion, clearly and efficiently. They deserve nothing less, because each of us, in our heart of hearts, wants to improve.

And each of us wants to tell others what we really are thinking. We want to communicate on the deepest level. When we fail to do so, when we know that we are holding back, we feel stress. It can be much more uncomfortable, in the long run, than speaking up. And in the long run, candor brings people closer. Some may fear it can wreck relationships—and yes, the immature may lash back at the very truth they purportedly sought out—but eventually it heals and strengthens relationships.

> *Some may fear it can wreck relationships—and yes, the immature may lash back at the very truth they purportedly sought out—but eventually it heals and strengthens relationships.*

The benefits of candor outweigh any potential costs. Once you become comfortable with candor and begin to practice it, it frees the mind. You're not constantly thinking about things left unsaid. Instead of pondering what you wish you had said and done, you can focus on more-productive thoughts. That's a much better use of your energy.

Once people begin to practice candor, they also see how much easier it is than dodging the truth and avoiding ticklish situations. People who begin to practice candor in the workplace tell me that they are actually having more fun at work.

Like anything else that you practice, you can develop the skills of candid conversation. Unfortunately, speaking up, quickly, with the facts and our beliefs is not a muscle that many of us have exercised. We may believe that we are being polite and warmhearted when we hold back the hard facts, but when we fail to be forthcoming we reveal a weakness. Those who need to hear the truth may wonder what else we are thinking. They have a natural skepticism and will sense when we are playing them—and that's what it can amount to. That's why it is so important not to hedge the truth. People will know. Those who truly want to be warmhearted will make it a habit to be straight with others.

> *Those who truly want to be warmhearted will make it a habit to be straight with others.*

If you are not forthright, then you could cause your company and your relationships a lot of harm. Without candor, people make the wrong decisions. The risks are more than personal. It can be costly to the team, to the organization, to the investors.

THE RIPPLE EFFECT

As those consequences ripple out, they affect one person after another, damaging productivity and eventually revealing themselves on the bottom line. Enhance your return on investment by enhancing the level of candor in your organization.

The president of a construction company gave me a prime example of how candor can boost the bottom line. His firm took over the rehab of a commercial property after the owner fired the first contractor. The timeline and budget had already been set, so the crew went right to work and resumed the project. At the owner's request, the construction company included $150,000 in the budget for future modifications to the new HVAC system that might be required by new tenants as they leased space in the building.

Months went by and the construction company completed all the tenant improvements without using any of the funds designated for the HVAC modifications. At the conclusion of the project, they discovered the unused funds and were fairly sure that their client had forgotten about it, as well. The construction company president had a decision to make. He could say nothing and keep the money (this "windfall" would have really helped the bottom line of his young company), or they could do the right thing and return the money. "It was an easy decision," the president said. "I brought the property owner a check for $150,000." The owner was surprised and confirmed that he had forgotten all about this money.

This honesty so impressed the owner that he spread the word about the construction company's integrity. "He must have given us fifty referrals and we probably got ten jobs from those referrals," the president told me. "We made that $150,000 at least ten times over."

SEEING THE WHOLE PICTURE

I have come to my father's point of view about what that optometrist said to him so long ago. The reason my father had gone to that town was to see how he would fit in there, and he found out. The optometrist clearly answered his question and gave his opinion when invited to do so, without holding back. To me, that's very honoring. I believe, as my father did, that those words—"Young man, you are Jewish, aren't you?"—were truly meant to be helpful.

Communication is in the giving and the receiving. We need to look at the whole: how the message is taken as well as how it is intended. We can misread intent, imagining things that aren't there, whether positive or negative. If we are in a bad relationship with someone, that person could say, "Good morning," and we would suspect ill will, but if we are in a good relationship, we see the best even when the words truly could be taken the wrong way. My father had worked side by side with this man all day long. In that time, they had developed a relationship that was open enough to afford the benefit of the doubt.

When all is well with our relationships, when we are open and communicating, we see the best in people. But without candor, things deteriorate. Even small problems and minor transgressions, if they are transgressions at all, feel magnified. It's true in friendships, it's true in families, and it's true in the workplace. And that is why a culture of candor is essential in all realms of life.

CHAPTER 2

WHAT CANDOR IS NOT

"A 'no' uttered from deepest conviction is
better and greater than a 'yes' merely uttered
to please, or what is worse, to avoid trouble."
—MAHATMA GANDHI

A COLLEAGUE OF MINE, a CEO and serial entrepreneur, was considering expanding her current business from the Mid-Atlantic into the Midwest, perhaps the Chicago area. She asked her leadership team to examine the market and prepare a presentation showing how this expansion could be successful and the steps they would need to take.

When the team members reported back in a few weeks time, they delivered a fantastic case for entering the new market. It was a detailed look at how the expansion would make a lot of sense.

However, the CEO noticed their arms were crossed and their brows furrowed. Their smiles seemed tense. Their demeanor didn't match the positive words in their presentation. So she finally stopped the presentation.

"Wait a minute," she said. "I really need to check in with you here. I'm hearing your words, but I'm not sensing excitement about this."

"What's up?"

One member of the leadership spoke on behalf of the others, "We don't think it's a good idea."

"Then, why are you telling me it's a good idea?" the CEO asked.

"Well, because you told us to bring you a presentation about expanding into this market. Sure, we can see how it can be done, but deep down we don't think it's the right move."

"Okay, but I also needed you to tell me if you thought it was a bad idea. Now tell me the reasons why it's not right for us." And when they did, she agreed with them. She didn't proceed with the expansion. The team had come out with the truth that the CEO wanted and needed to hear.

You have to be alert to the nonverbals, she later told me. Even if you believe you have an open and candid culture at your company, you have to be careful what you ask for. Your team still wants to please the boss. You need to leave the door open wide to all possibilities, or you risk that people will simply put a stamp on your ideas.

IT GOES BEYOND WORDS

"When the eyes say one thing, and the tongue another, a practiced man relies on the language of the first," Ralph Waldo Emerson wrote. He so eloquently reminds us that our actions speak louder than our words. How clichéd that may sound! And yet it's so true. Our body language can override the best attempts of our brains and our mouths.

We've long heard how facial expressions or posture will give away a lie. As my colleague observed, when people's true beliefs or feelings are out of sync with their words, their bodies betray them.

When delivering our messages, we must be sure that we are candid so that our nonverbal cues align with our statements. As the listener on the receiving end, weighing the nonverbal communications with equal importance allows us to gather the full picture. It's important to take note of the nuances of the conversation you're having. Does the body language match the message? If so, it's candor at its best. If not, ask questions.

When we want to understand the real deal, we have to look while we listen; when we want our truth to be heard, there's no dodging the issue. As we pursue candor in our work environments and within our relationships, our body language holds us, and those around us, accountable to the truth.

> *As we pursue candor in our work environments and within our relationships, our body language holds us, and those around us, accountable to the truth.*

THE "FEEDBACK SANDWICH"

It goes both ways. In an organization, candor must flow from the staff to the executive suite, and it also must trickle down from the top to permeate the culture. A company cannot make the best decisions unless its top leadership is alert to messages from below, as we have seen, but it also can get into trouble when the leaders themselves lack candor in dealing with their people.

Candor is not the "feedback sandwich" that managers sometimes advocate when giving performance evaluations. Typically, it goes like this: First, tell the employees what you think they do well. Then tell them where they need to develop, or what's missing, or what you believe they haven't delivered. And then wrap it up with what you like about their performance.

> Candor is not the "feedback sandwich" that managers sometimes advocate when giving performance evaluations.

As you can see, the direct statement you want to make ends up being sandwiched between two pieces of good news. That indeed might be the way to go in a full evaluation, but some managers do that even when they just want to impart a specific piece of information as feedback.

However, think about it from the perspective of those who receive such a communication. They hear two positives and just one negative and so, on balance, they figure they are doing fine. What people tend to recall from a conversation is what you say first and what you say last. They might not even hear what you say in the middle.

At best, that approach can be confusing. That middle message was what you wanted them to hear, and yet you placed it in the position of least importance. In communicating with employees, a supervisor is better off getting right to the middle.

CANDOR ISN'T BULLYING

I am a big fan of Jim Collins, author of *Good to Great* and *Great by Choice*. Collins tells us, "All great companies are brutally honest with themselves." I have often quoted him to emphasize how important it is to be candid in organizations.

Brutally honest? I understand what Collins and others are saying with this type of language. They are asking us to pull no punches, to confront the brutal facts. I agree wholeheartedly. Yet I am wondering if this tough language about sharing the facts and being forthright with our colleagues actually gets in the way of being candid.

Does language such as "brutally honest" fuel the notion that honesty is tough on others? Does it support the assessment that speaking the real deal will take great courage and, naturally, must be harsh and challenging? And that being direct with others is 180-degrees apart from respectful discourse and is not kind to others?

> *Real honesty, committed to someone's success, is never brutal.*

We need to see candor as talking openly or being curious, versus attacking or confronting our colleagues. Real honesty, committed to someone's success, is never brutal. It may be eye opening. It may be shocking. It may be a lot of things, but if brutal means hurtful or cruel, that's not the nature of candor.

Some people avoid conflict at any cost, and they don't bring up things that need to be said. Other people seem to relish conflict, and they bring up things that don't need to be said, or they bring them up in a harsh way. We must strike a balance. We must bring up what truly needs to be said, and we must do so constructively and never abusively.

Candor is not about beating anyone up. It is about straight talk. It is about communicating facts and observations and expectations. We all have times of anger, but think of this distinction: "That situation made me angry" versus "I am angry at you." These are normal feelings, but the message must never be delivered in a diminishing manner. If you focus on the facts of the situation, then you are less likely to go on a personal offensive.

To say, "You're an idiot," is not candor. Nor is, "You did a terrible job! When are you ever going to learn to do it right? We're losing this deal and it's all your fault." Those words tear down. They don't strive to build.

IT'S NOTHING PERSONAL

Candor is expressed like this: "I believe we weren't effective enough to get that deal. Let's look at the points where we might have done things differently for a better outcome." The conversation is not a personal attack. It's about the facts, what one likes or doesn't like, and how to proceed.

So much of communication is in the delivery. And if we deliver it in a responsible, mature way, we can motivate change without destroying relationships.

In lieu of a "You're an idiot" tirade, imagine saying this to your coworker as you walk out of a presentation meeting, "That didn't have the impact I'd hoped for. I think I should have [fill in the blank]. What do you wish you had done better?"

You encourage change with that approach. It says, "Let's put the conversation in the middle of the table and clarify all the things that we would do differently the next time." It's good to concede some role in the issue, even if it is only, "I'm concerned I didn't spell out clearly for you what I was looking for."

That opens the door to reflective conversation, at least if you're dealing with a mature person. "Hey, you're being big about this," he or she thinks, "so let me be big about this and let's actually talk about what we can do better here."

Candor doesn't sidestep. Ask yourself whether you have ever whispered to a colleague, "I just wish she would stop that nonsense!" or "It feels like he's never going to get a grip on what we need here." That's not candor. That's gossip. We all have had such moments, and I would hope the response would be, "So have you considered letting her know?" or, "Are you sure he's been told what we need?" It's a matter of showing honor and respect to people. If I were to talk to others about how I think someone needs to improve, why wouldn't I bring my thoughts directly to that person?

> *We need to seek out other people's impressions and perspectives, and we need to use plain and sincere language.*

CANDOR ISN'T CLOUDY

Clarity is the goal of candor, and we cannot reach it through either confrontation or concession. Communication requires balance. We need to seek out other people's impressions and perspectives, and we need to use plain and sincere language.

Candor helps us balance confrontation and concession, using the power of clarification. We are clarifying when we raise important issues for the purpose of everyone's progress. We are not going on an offensive, nor are we caving in. Neither extreme serves anyone well, and keeping the emphasis on clarification is the way to strike that balance.

A DIFFERENT APPROACH

Confront   Clarify   Concede

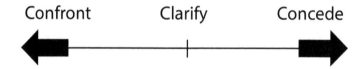

In matters big and small, clarity promotes understanding.

In late 2013, Mike Hughes, a leader with the Martin Agency based in Richmond, Virginia, passed away. In the last year of his illness, he wrote a blog, *Unfinished Thinking*, a string of beautiful and comedic musings that intrigued and inspired his readers. This posting struck me:

> *I want to help society address its big problems. I want to help righteous journalism maintain its integrity and its robustness. I want to figure out how to stop governments and politicians from getting in the way of progress. I want our schools to be better. I*

want scientists to learn how to talk to the rest of us so that all of us can get a firmer handle on the truth.

That last part about wanting scientists to learn how to talk to the rest of us so we can really understand stood out. If there were more clarity in the fields of science and medicine and the way that knowledge is communicated to the general public, then our ability to understand and cope would be so much more effective. The result would enable all of us to make clear judgments and decisions about health, our choices, and our world. Scientists know the truth about a lot of things, but they are so intent on being precise and giving us all the qualifiers that the information becomes difficult to process and understand. Maybe scientists and doctors think we can't understand, or maybe they assume we already do, but I agree with Mike in wishing they would tell things in a way that would help us grasp what we need to know.

> *Candor in science and medicine is not so much about needing to be more truthful; science is generally proven through expert research. It's about clarity.*

Candor in science and medicine is not so much about needing to be more truthful; science is generally proven through expert research. It's about clarity, and when the truth and clarity are combined, the impact is profound. Candor means that the experts are making it clearly understandable to the rest of us, the nonscientists, so we can use that knowledge to work our way through hard conversations. Whether it is climate change, the definition of "brain-dead," the value of the space program, or the facts about food safety, I am eager to hear the real deal. Uninformed lay people debating loudly in social and traditional media is no substitute for the facts from the scientists among us.

We should be grateful to hear the unadorned truth from others, in matters big and small. I recently gave some pretty direct feedback to a student who was taking a graduate class that I was instructing. I wrote my observation on the paper that the student had submitted, adding, "I hope you take this in the spirit of candor and commitment to your success that I intend it." He replied, via e-mail, "Actually, it felt a bit condescending."

I was delighted. After all, one of the lessons of that course was on the importance of candor. I had emphasized that we must let others know how things feel for us. In this case, how I had wanted to be heard was not how I was heard. So my intent did not match the impact. I called him to talk about it and clear things up. He wanted me to know that despite how I intended my words, "that's not how it was for me," and those class discussions on candor had encouraged him to respond. He didn't just shrug and ignore me. He was candid with me about my attempt at candor, and as a result, we had a rich conversation about how I might have handled it better, and how he could improve. His final grade reflected that.

Even those of us who have had plenty of practice at candor can still miss the mark. When we do, what we need is candor in return, and we can set things straight for the best results. Such are the dividends of being forthright with one another.

YOU CAN'T STAY IN YOUR CHAIR

A lapse in truth has its consequences. It's not just relationships that suffer from a lack of candor, but business prospects as well. By failing to effectively express ourselves, we risk losing opportunities or we take steps we should avoid. In other words, we cannot make our best decisions.

Consider what could have happened, for example, if that CEO colleague of mine had gone ahead and expanded into the Midwest. Suppose she hadn't noticed the body language of her team members, who signaled their belief that the expansion would be a bad idea.

"What if I had been meeting with my team by phone?" she told me. "What if I hadn't noticed how they really felt or decided not to look deeper into it? I might have expanded into a market, had my investors put a huge amount of money into a big distraction for the company, and seen it all flop. And it would all have been because we never got that clarity up front. I needed that candor. I always need it from them, about everything we do."

We can hurt our bottom line by not paying attention to what people really are thinking. It's important to not only hear their words but also to see their crossed arms and furrowed brows. That's all a huge part of communication. And to see it, you have to be there, and that means getting out of your chair and connecting with people.

CHAPTER 3

DOING UNTO OTHERS

*"Candor is a compliment; it implies
equality. It's how true friends talk."*
—PEGGY NOONAN

THE PHONE RANG AT MY DESK, and I heard my boss' voice: "Will you come to my office?"

"Sure," I said, because there really was nothing else to say. "What should I bring?"

"Nothing." It didn't exactly seem like a good sign.

I was one of three who reported directly to her. The four of us had decided how we would work together: We would fully discuss all issues that came up, debating the pros and cons together and then deciding on a course of action. If the majority felt we should go in a certain direction, we all would get on board with that decision and present a common front outside that room, even those of us who had initial misgivings.

Most of the time we agreed on everything. But not always. We had recently debated a topic and I favored Plan B, while the others backed

Plan A. After we hashed it out, I sincerely believed I was committed to the majority decision, and I thought I was communicating that to our associates.

I walked into her office and closed the door. My boss looked at me and said only this, "You are way too influential around here to not be with us 100 percent." Then she was silent.

I must have flushed. "I'm so sorry. I believed that I was." I felt mortified that she had seen the necessity of having this kind of conversation with me.

"Do I need to say anything else?" she asked.

"No, message received. Got it." I couldn't get out of there fast enough.

> *And I also came to realize that it can be honoring when people tell you that they can see through you.*

I learned this: If you are not 100 percent committed, it shows. Your lips might be saying one thing, but you will project an entirely different message.

And I also came to realize that it can be honoring when people tell you that they can see through you. In retrospect, that was a good day, and I respect her for calling me in.

Suppose she had chosen not to tell me that she had noticed I was not embracing that decision wholeheartedly. She could have decided it wasn't a big enough deal to mention. But if she noticed my lapse, then others no doubt noticed too, or soon would. My leadership ability would have been compromised, not just on that particular matter but also in other endeavors with the firm. I'd have had no clue as to why I lacked followers.

My boss gave me nothing less than a gift that day.

A GIFT TO TREASURE

It happens a lot: A supervisor sees something going awry, and figures, "Well, overall the employee does a really good job, so why bring up this little thing?"

Here's why: It might make all the difference in the world. To say nothing can hurt morale. To say nothing means you accept dysfunction, and when you do that, a small problem can develop into a big one. And to say nothing deprives an individual of an opportunity to improve. After that day, I stepped up the quality of my leadership. Candor helps groom people to be their best.

When someone gives you a gift, it is something to treasure. It's the better part of human nature to do for others

> *To say nothing can hurt morale. To say nothing means you accept dysfunction, and when you do that, a small problem can develop into a big one. And to say nothing deprives an individual of an opportunity to improve.*

what others have done for us. Once you recognize how you have benefited from candor, you can see the beauty in paying it forward.

Think of a time when someone spoke with candor to you about your performance. How do you feel about that person today? Did you feel that way at the time? Or did it take awhile to come around to understanding that it was for your own benefit? Perhaps it was life changing, or at least career changing.

I once put those very questions to a CEO who now owns a well-known company. He told me about his young whippersnapper days, when he was an ambitious salesman meeting all his goals. He also had a lot of ideas about how the company could be better run, and he was not shy about sharing them.

One day, the boss called him to his office, and the young man was pretty sure he was about to get a promotion.

"Do you know why you're here?" the boss asked.

"Well, I know you must like my work. I think you might be wanting to recognize my value, since I've shown myself to be a terrific salesman and have some great ideas about how things could work better here."

The boss peered at him. "Well, yes, I was going to mention all those ideas you seem to have. And you are indeed one of the best sales-people we've ever had."

"Yup."

"And you're fired."

The boss explained to the stunned young salesman that he had managed to irritate a lot of people at the company. "You need to stop telling us how to run this business, because that's not why we hired you."

"You do have a lot of ideas; it's true," he continued. "So let me tell you what I think you should do with them. You should go out and start your own business. You'll never make it in an organization like ours."

And the young salesman went out and did just that. "I might never have done it," he told me, "if that guy hadn't said, 'You'll never make it in an organization like ours.'"

I hear so many stories like that one. It's a theme. I spoke with a man who was an attorney heading a division in his law firm. He had come to Virginia after leaving a law firm in his home state of Ohio.

"What brought you to Virginia?" I asked him. He told me he had believed he was doing really well at his previous firm. He was on track to becoming a partner. In fact, he had done so well in attracting clients and bringing in revenue that he thought he might be considered for partner a year earlier than usual. He felt excited about the prospect when the decision time came and the senior partner called him in to his office.

"I know what you were hoping," the senior partner told him, "but we did not approve you this year."

"I understand," he replied. "I know it would have been early, so I'll just do what I've been doing, and we'll go for the normal timeline. There's always next year."

"No, there's not next year," the boss said. "Let me tell you. You will never make partner here. Not enough of the people who make this decision are your fans."

That forthright assessment, the attorney told me, was a gift, and one of the best he could have received. It spared him a wasted year. He left for a firm that wanted him to be a partner. Very often, he said, young lawyers and accountants who aspire to become partners are told, "Not this year." They don't hear the truth, which for some is, "Not ever, here."

A SERVICE TO OTHERS

Such stories lead me to reflect once again on the message that the optometrist gave to my father who had hoped to join him in Lynchburg, "I don't think it's likely that you will be successful here." In each case, those who heard a frank message ended up thinking of it as a gift. It motivated them to action and helped them to move forward.

Each of us has the capacity to be of great service to our fellow human beings. It's a matter of opening our hearts. Some people believe that opening your heart means kindness at all costs. Yes, one should be kind and tactful, but opening your heart means telling people what you know they need to know. Do that in a way that preserves relationships, without hiding the truth.

If the senior partner had let that young attorney continue to believe he might make partner, the law firm probably would have benefited from his hard work and ambition for another year or longer. Such candor actually might have been to the law firm's detriment. The boss could have rationalized that his reticence was kind, in that a young man with a family didn't need such bad news. But, instead, he chose to tell the whole truth.

> *So often, people take a paternalistic approach, deciding what is best for others.*

A POWERFUL QUESTION

So often, people take a paternalistic approach, deciding what is best for others. We shouldn't play God. The best we can do is to speak directly with clarity. We show our respect for others when we let them decide for themselves what is best and make sure they have the information they need to make the choices that are right for them.

It's not easy to be candid all of the time. It can be uncomfortable, but remember that you can change the course of people's lives simply by being forthright. Frankness must not flatten, of course. Nothing about candor should be harsh or aggressive or hurtful. But when you deliver the unvarnished truth with sensitivity, you are showing that you care.

If someone did that for you, why would you not do it for others? It's a powerful question. When we hold back our candor, we must consider whether we are trying to protect ourselves more than we are the other person. Are we really in a position to make decisions on what people can handle? "Ignorance is bliss," the saying goes, which I counter with this: An informed decision is best.

> *Are there people who need your forthright advice so that they can grow?*

Think again about those who have helped you, not only in your career but also in your life, by revealing to you a truth that others had ignored or concealed and that you may have been hiding from yourself. A gift like that shouldn't stop with you. Are there people who need your forthright advice so that they can grow? There's no reason to wait. Your time is now.

CHAPTER 4

"I WISH YOU HAD TOLD ME!"

"Be who you are and say what you feel,
because those who mind don't matter
and those who matter don't mind."
—ANONYMOUS

I REMEMBER CHEERING for Marion Jones during the 2000 Olympic track and field events in Sydney, when she became the first woman to win five gold medals in a single Olympics. I knew that she was inspiring women around the world.

While many hailed her as "the fastest woman on the planet," some believed Jones may have used performance-enhancing drugs leading up to her Olympic success. She admitted to the drug use and subsequently relinquished all five medals. She went to jail for six months for initially lying to federal prosecutors.

I kept thinking, "What went wrong? How did this happen? What made her decide to use drugs when she had so much going for her?"

Piers Morgan of CNN spoke with Jones about her life before and after jail. He asked the same questions that had troubled me. She admitted that she only surrounded herself with people who told her how great she was. As a result, she pushed away the people who would challenge what she was doing. She distanced herself from her mother, the only person she knew would give it to her straight. Jones was afraid of what her mother would say and, therefore, avoided any contact with her.

Have you ever been afraid to talk to someone you care about (and who you know cares about you) because you were sure that person wouldn't agree with what you were doing? Have you ever avoided those who you believe may challenge your thinking?

> *Make sure that those around you will tell you the real deal about whatever you're going through, whether it's personal or work related, whether you are succeeding or failing.*

Jones now tells young people, "When you get advice, make sure it's from people who will give it to you straight." Her story reminds me how important it is to surround ourselves with people who are not afraid to be candid.

Jones says she has come to recognize that she gathered people around her who just kept making her feel as if whatever she did was great. When you're starting to win and you're in the public eye, you draw a lot of people who are like groupies. They tell you that whatever you want to do is a great idea.

Jones said that when she started on steroids, she knew her mother would disapprove, and so she distanced herself. Her lesson now, in particular for children and young adults, is this: Make sure that those around you will tell you the real deal about whatever you're going through, whether it's personal or work related, whether you are succeeding or failing.

It's all about being accountable. We don't want to be surrounded by "yes" people. So often, people behave like a master marionette, with puppets nodding at their behest. They are accountable to nobody, and as a result, they spiral downward. What can pick them up is being with somebody who has the strength and caring to tell it like it is.

> *We don't want to be surrounded by "yes" people.*

One of my mentors from the Georgetown Leadership Coaching program coined a statement that I love: "We often are upset about the results we never got to the requests we never made." That's the theme in the Marion Jones experience: If you aren't looking for something, you have no reason to be upset that you don't get it.

We make so many assumptions. Sometimes we think that others should just know what we want or need, as if we shouldn't have to make a request out loud, because people should just read our minds or think exactly like we do. Or we figure that others already know what we should tell them, and therefore we keep our silence. As models for living, those assumptions are far from efficient and can be dangerous if others are unaware of the peril or unwilling to warn us about it.

THE TRUTH ABOUT WASTED TIME

A business consultant in the real estate community once told me that he had been grateful for a new perspective on a situation. He had been named head of a company tax division. The division had been losing money, and at his initial meeting with his new team and colleagues in the company, the talk about the tax division was all gloom and blame. He returned to his office, furious at the attitudes and thoroughly discouraged.

His phone rang. It was another division head, asking to stop in for a visit. They chatted, and the visitor said, "I don't know what you are going to do, but let me tell you what I see. The tax division has never been run as a meaningful part of our firm. It has always been viewed as an adjunct to another division." It was the perspective the tax chief needed to hear. Knowing that it had been run as the stepchild to another company entity and not as an important profit center all these years gave him a fresh view of how to be successful in his new role.

"That simple statement," he told me, "gave me all new possibilities, opened my eyes, made me focus on ABC, not DEF, not just trying to improve on the status quo, but giving me a fundamentally new start. It taught me that when we are 'close in' to a situation, we focus, and that can be good. But it also means we can't see the broader view that others, who are not close in, need to show us. He probably saved me two years of unproductive work."

As a consultant today, he is highly regarded in the real estate community, and he says he is known for being forthright about what he sees. He deeply appreciates those helpful words from a colleague, and the experience added to his belief in candor.

I know how that feels, although my own experience was less uplifting. I was a general manager responsible for a startup business unit within an established organization, although it wasn't part of the core business. We had set some targets and were delighted to be exceeding them for the year. It was May or June, and we were doing really well.

"Are you feeling good about where we are?" I asked the owner as he arrived at the office one day.

"Well," he said, "I'd really like to see, by the end of the year, that you have doubled the results that you forecasted for the year."

I was quite taken aback because I thought we were running really hard. We had been trending about 20 percent ahead of budget. But to be 100 percent ahead of budget seemed a little out of bounds. I couldn't imagine how we would get there.

So I asked him, "Can you tell me why you want to see that? Is there something in the marketplace that makes you think the timing is better than when you set the budget?"

"No," he said. "It's just what I want you to do."

So we worked hard. I was getting a little afraid, because I didn't know what was driving that request. I began to think that his motive was to offset losses from a couple of business units. In other words, he was pushing us so that he could meet his total company budget numbers.

"Why aren't you talking to them?" I finally said the next time we met. "Are you trying to get me to be the rising tide that floats all boats?"

"No," he replied. "Their success or failure has nothing to do with how you're running your business."

"All right then," I said. "So can you please tell me if there's something I'm not doing right or I'm missing?" I kept probing but just couldn't get an answer. I felt it was a mistake to have brought it up. As a final offer, I even suggested he might get a new leader for the division, as I couldn't see how to hit the new goal. He assured me he was not going to replace me.

By November, we were still ahead of the original budget by 20 percent, but clearly, we were not going to come in at 100 percent over. I told him that I didn't know what else to do to close out the year and hit that revised goal, and that I was still perplexed.

At that point he told me that his board had informed him in May that unless we got to that new stretch goal, he should spin off the division and get it out of the holding company, since it was not part of the core business.

"Why didn't you tell me?" I asked. I had thought all along that something was wrong with me.

"I thought it would scare you," he said. The irony was that I couldn't have been more scared as a result of his lack of candor. I wasn't an entry-level employee. I was a general manager, and I had been asking for some kind of explanation.

People sometimes withhold information from us when they think we just don't need to know. They may feel it will scare us, or slow us down, or distract us. But instead, it is their silence that ends up doing all those things. His impact was the opposite of his intent. If I had been privy to what he was thinking, I likely would have suggested that we find a buyer for that unit immediately. We would have been in an entirely different conversation.

> *People sometimes withhold information from us when they think we just don't need to know. They may feel it will scare us, or slow us down, or distract us. But instead, it is their silence that ends up doing all those things.*

When we don't talk about such matters and withhold information, we're not doing anybody or anything any good, including the bottom line. When people understand an organization's goals and mission, and where the leaders are planning to take it, they are far more likely to get on board.

You likely can think of times in your own life and career when you have heard information that you wished you had known earlier. Perhaps, you too will see that it could have made all the difference in the world.

WHAT WE DO IN LIEU OF CANDOR

Whenever I ask clients what they do instead of taking the candid approach, I hear similar answers. They often tell me that they keep rehearsing the conversation, trying to figure out just how they are going to make their point, and never seem to get there. They delay and avoid. Or they tell somebody else about the situation instead of talking directly to the one who needs to know and who, perhaps, even asked for feedback.

It can get to the point where we resent those whom we have not told how we feel. They continue to behave or do things the same way, clueless about what is expected of them. We offer no direction, yet expect people to know the way. Does that make sense?

Each of us needs others to hold us accountable, and if we are to hold others accountable, we need to at least tell them what we think, with clarity and tact. That is a principle to live by, whether in the office or in the home.

If you come home two days in a row and find dirty dishes in the sink, for example, you might think, "I would only do that to someone I didn't care about." So you ascribe your own feelings to your roommate or spouse or whomever you live with. You figure that person doesn't care about you. But you don't come right out with the matter at hand: "So what's with the dishes these days?" Chances are, the answer will not be, "Oh, that? I just wanted to demonstrate how I don't care about you."

If you ask about troubling situations at home or at work, it's likely you will find an acceptable explanation, if you are open to hearing it. The person involved simply might not have been feeling well, or was struggling with something. Or you might uncover a genuine misunderstanding about household roles, or office roles.

That's far better than imagining something that's far from the real deal. When we have expectations and someone isn't abiding by them, it is a mistake to jump to a conclusion. The best way to learn another's motives is to ask him or her outright.

When I meet with groups, I sometimes start off by asking how many people have teenagers at home, or have raised teenagers, or have been a teenager. Then I say, "Okay, here's the scenario. You have told your child to take out the garbage daily. Each day you come home and it hasn't moved. So what do you conclude?" I hear such comments as, "The kid is lazy," and, "She doesn't love us," and even, "He'll never amount to anything." And the only fact we have is that the trash is still in the kitchen.

We can do so much damage by not communicating clearly. Sure, teenagers need high standards, but they are maturing and patience is importance. They need to cooperate, but adults who make caustic comments about their worth will compound the problem a hundredfold. Some people walk through life wounded because of what frustrated parents have said and done. And if it happens in families, you know it happens in workplaces. People wound each other unnecessarily by lack of clarity.

When we ascribe motivations to people without talking to them about how they feel, we are on a collision course. As frustrations build, communication can descend into brow beating, nagging, or silence. It happens in families, and it happens in businesses.

CLARIFYING CONVERSATIONS

It just makes sense that if we expect certain behaviors, we first have to request them and then explain what we mean. Still, some people find it so hard to talk about such things that they just do the task themselves, grumbling all the while. They write that proposal themselves, or they take out that garbage. It's good to stand firm. If you give up and take the garbage out yourself, you will just hear your voice getting louder to the point where you're at risk of apoplexy. Instead of yelling, talk about your differing views. That's one good way to a solution.

> *It just makes sense that if we expect certain behaviors, we first have to request them and then explain what we mean.*

A workaround is no solution. It doesn't promote productivity. An employer expects the best of everyone who is hired. You defeat that goal when you find ways to get the job done without the input that you need from someone else. Resentful, you find yourself looking for evidence of that person's failings, as if you were building a case for incompetence. Further, when you relegate that person to minor tasks or peripheral duties unrelated to the true talents that could be developed in him or her, you waste potential.

Clarifying conversations are a far better alternative, but people often tell me they don't have time for them. To that, I suggest they keep a timesheet for a week to track how many hours they spend in a swirl around what is not working—that is, time spent in unproductive thought, in anger, frustration, and workarounds. You get a new perspective when you think of these problems as time eaters.

One way to put a stop to such a lack of productivity is to fire the unproductive person rather than drag out the situation, but that's terribly shortsighted if you haven't even had a conversation about what needs to change. Together, perhaps, you could easily find a way to overcome the problem. You may discover other talents or skills for which the employee is better suited, and offer training in a wholehearted attempt to develop those abilities. In other words, you could help to provide what is missing—if you find out what that is.

> *An employee with a problem deserves clarity. The manager will do well to either explain what it means to be successful and help the employee get there, or tell the employee that it's time to part company.*

So often, managers opt for expedience. We have so much work to do and only so much time to do it in. We protest that holding somebody's hand isn't part of the job description. Yet, working for the benefit of the organization to improve the bottom line is part of everyone's job description, and making the most of human potential is how that happens.

An employee with a problem deserves clarity. The manager will do well to either explain what it means to be successful and help the employee get there, or tell the employee that it's time to part company.

"YOU WILL NOT STAND IN THE WAY"

I once attended a speech by Colin Powell to high schoolers, parents, and alumni of an independent school. Somebody asked him why he went into the military. He explained that he entered not too long after the U.S. Army had been desegregated. As a black man embarking on a military career, he was told that if he performed well, he would do well. Powell was not sure that would have been the case in other organizations/institutions at that time. I thought these were remarkably candid statements.

When he did advance to positions of authority in the military, he was frank with those who were not making the grade. "I can move you, I can train you, or I can demote you," Powell said he told them. "But you will not stand in the way of the progress of this division."

Those are commanding words from a position of strength. They communicate this: "You have a few choices here, but one of them will not be to hold us back." Every CEO and every leader in any organization would do well with that kind of attitude, even if those words might make some human resource professionals shiver. People need to know where they stand, that they have choices, and that you will work with them, up to a reasonable point.

It can be a fine line to walk. Our society has checks and balances to help prevent abuses of power, such as arbitrary firings by a malicious manager. Many workers have union protection, with contracts that specify the boundaries of managerial power. History has shown abuses of corporate power, in which workers have been used and discarded and have fought hard for dignity and security.

Ultimately, the way to dignity and security is to make sure we all are held accountable, managers and employees. When we can identify situations that have gone awry, we can move toward rectifying them. The flow of clear, candid communication within an organization helps us to do that.

THE COSTS OF THE LACK OF CANDOR

When we think of the risks of candor, we sometimes worry about hurting others' feelings. Seldom do we consider how we will hurt people if we don't come out with what needs to be said. Lacking feedback, people might decide on one of two very different things: "Everything must be fine," or "Nobody cares. How I do things doesn't matter."

> *A lack of candor keeps people in the dark and deprives them of a learning experience that would help them to advance in their careers.*

A lack of candor keeps people in the dark and deprives them of a learning experience that would help them to advance in their careers. They may even misinterpret your silence to mean you agree with their position or are content with their efforts, when you are thinking something entirely different. That's why they may be quite surprised when you, or somebody else, finally talks straight with them. Hopefully, you haven't wasted too much of their time.

Personally, I know that if I'd not had these great people in my world, who have given me good feedback, I would not have accomplished some of the things that have been meaningful to me in my career and my personal life. I'm very grateful.

In the case of U.S. Supreme Court Justice Sonia Sotomayor, candor had the power to move a career from already pretty great to truly extraordinary.

Sotomayor has achieved what most would say is unbelievable. Statistically speaking, the chance of becoming one of the very few who are selected and confirmed to the high court is highly unlikely. And yet, Sotomayor is the court's one hundred and eleventh justice, its third female and first Hispanic. It might make one wonder which specific, unique factors contributed to her success.

In her autobiography, *My Beloved World*, Sotomayor tells the story of her childhood through the early years of her career.

She describes a particular moment that demonstrates her drive for continuous improvement. While serving in the district attorney's office in the county of New York, Sotomayor lost two trials in succession. She went to bureau chief Warren Murray and asked him to help her discover what went wrong:

> *"Okay. Tell me what you did," Warren said.*

> *I walked him through my presentation of both cases.*

> *He identified the problem instantly: I was appealing to logic, not morality, and, in effect, letting the jury off the hook. Since it is painful to most jurors to vote "guilty" and send a human being to jail, you couldn't simply reason with them to do it; you had to make them feel the necessity.*

> *"They have to believe they have a moral responsibility to convict," Warren said.*

Sotomayor says this insightful response dramatically changed how she argued cases and calls this the "single most powerful lesson" she would ever learn. She never lost another case. And this breakthrough (as she calls it) came from her willingness to be vulnerable, to ask for help, to admit she was struggling, and to be receptive to her boss' direct feedback.

Imagine the cost to her, and to our country, if her bureau chief had just shrugged at her setback.

In interviews, she tells many anecdotes about asking for feedback.

When she learned she was going to have the opportunity to throw a ceremonial first pitch at a Yankees game, she went into the courtyard where she was working and practiced every day, throwing the ball to home plate, knowing everyone could see her and leaving herself vulnerable and open to pointers. She has no qualms about appealing for help and advice so that she can get better. It has been a hallmark of her career.

It's a lesson for us all: Focusing on candor, asking for honest feedback from those you respect and embracing their insight can work for you, as it has worked for one of our newest justices. Think of your own career, and your own life: How has candor impacted your path, or the paths of those connected to you? Has the lack of it been costly to you? Are there conversations that might make a difference for your career?

THE "NO-SPIN" ZONE

Shawn H. Wilson is a deep believer in straight talk. He is president of Usher's New Look Foundation, which is dedicated to developing youth leadership. His office, he says, is a place where nobody is allowed to make excuses or spin the facts.

Adam Bryant, "Corner Office" columnist for the *New York Times* (and author of a book by the same name), interviewed Wilson about his leadership experiences and lessons learned.

In the interview, Bryant notes that, at New Look, Wilson is nicknamed "the godfather" and is known for the "godfatherisms" that he regularly dispenses. For example, he talks about balancing fierce ambition and due patience. He believes it takes a lot of time to build a shared vision in an organization.

When the columnist prodded Wilson for another godfatherism, he replied:

> *I always tell my staff, "When you come in my office, you're in a no-spin zone. Just be respectful." I've seen the habit in other organizations and I saw it creeping into our organization, where people tend to make excuses or spin the truth.*

Wilson said he decided that leaders in his organization needed to get to the core root, the underlying facts, of why something happened. They can't accept excuses or unfounded explanations. "When we started that," he told Bryant, "I definitely saw a difference in the culture."

Wilson reminds us that candor is uncommon enough that we need to declare our desire for it. Do we follow his lead when it comes to requesting the straight story when we want it?

I wonder how often we assume we are getting the forthright accounting of events when we are not. How many bad decisions are made and how much time is wasted? How often will we have to say, "I wish you had told me!"

We all would do well to post a "no-spin zone" sign on our office doors. It's unfortunate that we have to remind people to be forthright when they enter our

> *We all would do well to post a "no-spin zone" sign on our office doors.*

office, but it's so hard to persuade people to be candid. It should be the easiest way to communicate, but we let ourselves get in the way. And as a result, important messages are never heard, and important changes don't happen.

FINDING THE SAFE ZONE

Sometimes, to avoid the spin, you have to depend on a circle of people you know well and trust. A good friend and colleague once observed that as we collaborated on a project, I seemed different; I was not my best self, let's just say. He could have just brushed it off, but here's how he broached the matter with me: "You know, Nancy, you do this better than 99 percent of the people, but for the last couple of weeks I think you've been very impatient with me." I had to respect that. He told me his impression clearly, while also letting me know that I mattered to him. He was so right. I had been impatient with others, too. I got a good attitude adjustment, and I was honored that he felt safe with me in saying that.

He didn't presume that I had it in for him. He didn't start doubting himself. He just asked me what was up. It gave me the opportunity to be understood, to sincerely explain what I was going through, and it gave me a chance to change. To be heard, and to better ourselves, isn't that what we all desire?

I talked to the CEO of a major law firm in February 2009, about a year into the recession. He told me that candor is particularly essential during economic crisis, and he explained that he had to seek out the people who he knew would give him the truth without any spin.

Some had suggested that he reassure the partners and associates that everything would be just fine, but he felt that was giving false hope when, in truth, he couldn't say whether things would be okay.

He told his firm that it was time to face the fear and take action.

> I told them, "If you are not scared, then you are not paying attention. We cannot control the economic environment, but let's begin to control what we can control. Let's do great things with our colleagues. Let's do excellent work for our clients. Let's bring joy to each other when things may not feel joyful. Let's not hunker down but, rather, get in conversation about how to grow and improve in this tough time."

> I have certain colleagues who provide safe zones for me. As I am a CEO, not everyone will be straight with me. So I have to go to

small groups or individuals and ask them for the real deal. I need to talk particularly with colleagues who give me a reality check, versus being spun. I need good data to make good decisions. You have to invite it, welcome it, thank them for it and then thank them again for it, and still it's hard to get people to do it.

I tell people I want us to be a culture of learning, not blame. Here's what we did wrong so that we know what to do better next time. We do a confidential 360-degree feedback. I am reviewed by 39 colleagues and the survey questions include what are people afraid to tell the CEO? What should the CEO stop doing? What should the CEO start doing? And then when I hear it, I must accept it, not argue with it—and learn from it. The only bad question is the one you failed to ask. We have a system where people can, if they choose to, give me questions with no name attached. So if I'm looking for good data, I want it in whatever format I can get it. I have made too many mistakes when I haven't probed enough, been empathetic enough, or acted too quickly without the information.

> **The only bad question is the one you failed to ask.**

He told me about a colleague who he felt was a model of candor. Upon finishing a project, the colleague always said, "I'm satisfied that we did a hundred things right here, and we'll be working together for a long time, but now let's talk about the three things I want us to do better next time."

The upfront message there is "I value you," first and foremost, and in that context any criticism becomes constructive for the purpose of valuing you even more. It builds rather than diminishes. It encourages the kind of communication that makes it unnecessary to have to say, "I wish you had told me!"

CHAPTER 5

SHARING OUR VULNERABILITIES

"The most exhausting thing in
life is being insincere."
—ANNE MORROW LINDBERGH

"NANCY, I WANT TO HAVE A TALK WITH YOU. Please come to my office."

The call was from the CEO of a bank, a $10 billion enterprise where I was head of a product development division. I did not report directly to the CEO, so it was unusual for me to get such a call without my immediate boss being included.

I called her at once to let her know that the CEO had summoned me to his office.

She simply said, "Yes."

"Should I prepare anything?"

"No. You should just go."

Notebook in hand, I arrived at his office. He proceeded to tell me that the regional president for the northern region—a portfolio worth about $1 billion—was retiring. I scribbled down everything he was telling me, certain that he was preparing to ask for a product launch in honor of the retiree's replacement.

Then I heard him say, "I'd like you to take over that job upon his retirement." I stopped taking notes.

I just looked at him, wondering what to say, and this is what I came up with: "You know I have never underwritten a loan in my life."

The CEO, who had progressed to his position through the investments department of the bank, leaned forward in his chair. "Neither have I."

Those words have stayed with me for many years because I felt a sense of freedom at that moment. "So what you're telling me is that I should go up there and make sure I'm surrounded by the right people who can get the job done."

"Exactly."

About two weeks later, the CEO died.

My promotion had not been announced. I didn't even know whether his successor as CEO agreed with him and wanted me to be the regional president, but it turned out that he did, and I assumed my new role.

In the weeks and months ahead, I kept thinking of those three words ("Neither have I") as I strived to hit the goals that my departed leader had set for me that day in his office. We had hit it off, and though he could not be there in my corner to support me in my new endeavor, I felt his presence over and over again. Whenever I faced something new to me, I could see past the details and embrace how my leadership could influence the outcome. I knew what really mattered.

He had seen in me more than my past performance. My immediate thought had been, "I don't know if I can do this," a common and very human fear.

We all have moments like that, when we don't know whether we are up to the task. Why don't we express them? Think about a time when you have held back in expressing your own fears and doubts. Why did you hesitate? Were you worried that you would look bad, or weak?

> *People often tell me they're worried that people will unmask them or find out that the emperor has no clothes.*

People often tell me they're worried that people will unmask them or find out that the emperor has no clothes. They even tell me they have this dream in which people are looking behind a curtain and discovering what's really there, as if they're a sham or a fraud.

To me, to have that dream means not that you are hiding your failure but that you are challenging yourself to go beyond where you are comfortable. You are developing and growing as you move into a territory where you haven't been before.

TELLING OUR STORY

We nonetheless worry about expressing our vulnerabilities, and the root of that hesitation often goes back deep into childhood. People dredge up old insecurities, or they hear, again, words that were drummed into them time after time, usually subtly, and occasionally cruelly. They react, sometimes, by projecting an overconfidence that admits no weakness. They may feel that admitting their vulnerabilities will expose them. What often happens, however, is that the sharing actually opens opportunities as people bond with one another in their common humanity.

Michelle McKenna, chief information officer of the National Football League, knows what it is like to be a woman and a working mother in the male-dominated worlds of technology and football. Her career choices have been challenging and her decisions have led her on an interesting path.

In her speaking engagements, she addresses the importance of communication, and she is referring to a lot more than meetings and memos. She means actually talking to people, having conversations and, sometimes, tough ones. Often, this kind of candid conversation may unsettle the human resources or legal departments, she says, and yet it is of utmost importance.

Recently, McKenna interviewed a woman whom she was very eager to hire and bring on the team. She believed the woman might be at the stage of her career where she would be wondering about having children while taking on the job.

McKenna wasn't certain whether that played a role in the woman's consideration of the job, but she openly addressed the possibility. "Let me tell you my story," she said, and went on to share how she juggled her travel and out-of-state office location with the schedules of her children and with help and support from the other adults in their lives. Her family is in Florida and she is in New York for most of the week, and she explained how supportive the NFL had been in helping her to manage that situation.

For whatever reason, whether to be politically correct, or because of our litigious society, we hold back, sometimes, from even saying what is true for ourselves.

"We just have to tell our stories," McKenna says. It might seem a very personal point on which these two professionals were relating, and yet it was a complex career concern that they had to address. McKenna says that as she interviewed the woman, she kept imagining herself at that age and the concerns that would have been going through her head. One of them might have been, "Will I be able to manage a job like this if I decide to have children?"

Though she did not ask the woman whether she, too, had such concerns, McKenna decided to relate her own experience. For whatever reason, whether to be politically correct, or because of our litigious society, we hold back, sometimes, from even saying what is true for ourselves.

Her openness paid off. The candidate accepted the job and told her that a deciding factor was when McKenna shared her own experience in managing family and career. This reminds us that candor can happen at unexpected moments and have a significant impact. If we make it a habit to tell our stories, openly and honestly, we are able to create connections that grow opportunities for ourselves and those around us.

WHEN CANDOR OFFENDS

For all its benefits, candor doesn't always go over well. Outspoken and forthright people, even when they show all due respect, sometimes encounter enmity among those who simply don't wish to hear it or feel they need to protect others from harm. Authors who have candid messages can even find themselves the target of attempts to ban their books, as has been the case for Phyllis Reynolds Naylor.

> *Outspoken and forthright people, even when they show all due respect, sometimes encounter enmity among those who simply don't wish to hear it or feel they need to protect others from harm.*

Naylor has written a series of books about a girl named Alice growing up in Silver Spring, Maryland. Naylor's books have been targeted for more bans than any other books this past decade, according to a recent article about her in *The Washington Post*. The Alice book series is often on the American Library Association's annual list of top ten books that groups or individuals have tried to get removed from library shelves or classrooms—more often than the Harry Potter series of books and *The Hunger Games*, which some say promote witchcraft and violence. Yet Alice is just your average girl, dealing with very normal schoolgirl challenges, in the series that follows her from age 12 to 18.

So, what's the rub with Alice? What's so awful that many believe these books have to be hidden from young readers? Not much at all, really, except that Naylor's candor about the physical and emotional maturation of girls is terribly uncomfortable for many. In her series, Alice deals with everything from bad haircuts to how babies are made, and many other topics that parents may fear talking about with their daughters.

> *Naylor's books have been targeted for more bans than any other books this past decade.*

In *The Washington Post* article, Naylor explains why she thinks her books are banned: "I think the fear is that the child is going to come to them and ask them questions that feel too personal," Naylor said. "It's not that their child's not ready. It's that they're not ready. I've had a lot of letters from people saying, 'Oh, my daughter doesn't even *know* about that,' and I can only think, ha-ha."

Candor is always hardest when addressing important, uncomfortable, or sensitive subjects, but that's when it's most needed. Practicing candor with the easy things helps. Then, we have to set aside our fears and stay on the path of being open and honest in the hardest conversations.

We learn candor from our authority figures, and these mentors shape us long before we enter the boardroom. When children are open to talking about important matters, adults should take this as a cue to listen carefully before the moment passes.

TEARING DOWN THE FENCES

Children are transparent creatures. From an early age, they often pretty much say whatever comes into their heads, to the point where the grownups often feel compelled to shush them. "You can't say that," some parents say, scowling, or "That's not nice." That's the case even if the child is speaking the truth. Seldom do adults use words that communicate this to a child: "Yes, you are correct, but let's find a more respectful way to say it."

> *We learn candor from our authority figures, and these mentors shape us long before we enter the boardroom.*

We begin to put fences around what we can say. By the time we get to be adults, we've been given a lot of direction on what we shouldn't say, but not much guidance on how to be candid in a respectful and honoring way. The adult wants the child to be tactful and always show respect. The child ends up punished for saying something and gets the message that he or she should just shut up at all costs. That's a mindset that is shaped early and could stay with someone for a lifetime. Some people clam up around authority figures.

Parents want to train their children not to come across as blunt and cruel, but it is important, as well, not to thwart communication. That, too, requires a parent's influence. Most parents want their children to stand up for themselves. They want their children to feel free to tell an adult when something doesn't feel right or when something bad may be happening. Wise parents know that if that's what they want, they must teach their children well.

Some people struggle for years with messages they have hung on to since childhood. Their fears and doubts hold them back. Children start out, like Little Red Riding Hood, with candor: "Grandmother, what big teeth you have!" And, like her, they find that their expression of candor doesn't necessarily bring them to a happy ending.

A CHILD'S NATURAL CANDOR

Rather than bare your teeth, it's far better to encourage a child's natural candor. I have a friend who is raising two girls. Mother and daughters talk openly about a lot of things. One day, I was at their house and one of the girls, who was about nine years old, was trying to do her homework. Her mother kept asking her how her day had gone, and the girl felt frustrated at the persistent questioning. She looked at her mom and said, "I think this is not a good time for me to give you an answer." My friend said to her, "Okay, got it," and her daughter went back to her work, and that was the end of the conversation.

If I had felt such frustration at that age, I probably would have cried and called my mother a name (under my breath, of course) and left the room. How did this child develop that skill? I have a feeling that she got some feedback early on, telling her she need not get mad, or pout, or go silent, but just explain what's going on with her. She just told her mother how she was feeling, clearly and candidly, and yet it was surprising to witness. And what a concept! We can just put our feelings into words, instead of throwing our toys around.

Yet, many adults squelch that natural candid instinct when they see it in children because it makes them feel uncomfortable. They deem certain knowledge unacceptable and try to protect children from it. Meanwhile, the children become intrigued and whisper among themselves about how to learn more about that forbidden knowledge.

As children lose their innocence, adults direct them to "do this, don't do that."

> *They may never share the poetry in their hearts, or the unspeakable pain that someone has inflicted.*

Our society has much to gain by encouraging the outgoing nature of children and much to lose in abiding by the old dictate that they are to be seen, not heard. By silencing them, grownups squelch their creativity or make them fearful of expressing their troubles. They may never share the poetry in their hearts, or the unspeakable pain that someone has inflicted. And when those children grow up, they are likely to carry that reticence into their families and into their workplaces. If, instead, we tell young people to talk about it and that together we'll figure it out, no matter what, then that's the attitude they will carry forth. The candor will spread.

I volunteer to spend two eight-hour shifts a month with a group that goes to emergency rooms to meet patients who have reported domestic violence or sexual assault. We act as their advocate there. What has often struck me is the shame these patients feel. That's frequently one of the first emotions they express, as if they somehow were responsible for what happened to them, or it was their fault. They have been violated, but they point the finger at themselves, believing that others surely will, as well.

Those are dire circumstances, but that mindset is widely manifested. Family secrets can remain for decades in the dark because nobody will talk about what really happened. When candor is lacking, the wrong people can suffer.

A CURE FOR HARRY'S HANG-UP

Consider the following profile and whether any element of it might apply to someone you know: Fearful of hurting anyone's feelings, Harry shrinks from straight talk. He feels that people perhaps won't like him for who he really is, so he puts on an act. If people do like him, it's not the real Harry they like. He might as well be a player in a script. Others can sense that he is putting on a spin, and they doubt his sincerity.

> *When candor is lacking, the wrong people can suffer.*

Harry might have felt that hiding his full true self would help his relationships, but it did quite the opposite. He kept people at a distance, and others noticed and kept their own distance. The more he avoided being open and vulnerable, the more aloof and disconnected he felt.

In the workplace, such shallow relationships among coworkers can stifle ideas and growth. If candor is not part of the culture, people might come to believe that any criticism of an initiative will be like throwing the boss or a colleague under the bus. They would rather be silent than hurt anyone's feelings or risk alienating anyone.

It is difficult for a leader to make changes in such a culture. Savvy leaders understand that a good way to make inroads is to model their own vulnerability. They admit their mistakes, and talk about how they now want to do things differently for everyone's benefit. They confess their doubts. Others observe their openness and feel safe to be vulnerable themselves, and in that way, in time, everyone does indeed benefit. No longer are they a crew of "yes" people, nodding like puppets. They will speak up about their concerns, and suggest better ways. They will tell it like it is.

> *Savvy leaders understand that a good way to make inroads is to model their own vulnerability.*

AN INSPIRATION FOREVER

I think, again, about those three words that the bank CEO said when I confessed that I had never underwritten a loan: "Neither have I." He didn't try to convince me that I could do it. You can't convince people to change their perspective, as any good salesperson knows. They decide for themselves. If he had told me all the reasons why he thought I could handle the promotion, I'm not so sure I would have said yes to the job. It may have felt like too much of a climb for me in a new market, doing things I had never done before, with 400 employees speaking 26 different languages. I might have said, "No, thank you."

As it turned out, I loved making loans. I felt that I was helping people to realize their dreams, whether for a family home or for their business.

In making loans, I got to know people by listening to their stories. I was candid with them, and it was clear to me when they were being candid in return. I found that I had a sense for when people were upfront about their intentions and commitments.

No doubt the CEO could see how it would all work out. He was confident in me. But he wanted me to be confident in myself, and he knew that being vulnerable, and sharing a truth about himself, would be most compelling. It was unusual in 1995, in Virginia, for a woman to be a regional bank president. On my first day, I heard from female tellers from around the state—we had 3,500 employees— who appreciated knowing they could aspire to such a position. A lot of women in our organization felt encouraged, but I was thinking more about living up to the show of faith. I wanted to demonstrate my gratitude.

Today, I think of that long-gone soul. Because he shared, I could grow.

CHAPTER 6

"YOU'VE BEEN TALKING TO WILSON"

"Right up front, tell people what you're trying to accomplish and what you're willing to sacrifice to accomplish it."
—LEE IACOCCA

I WAS PROUD OF MYSELF as I marched into the CEO's office to give my whiz-bang presentation.

My boss, Josh Freeman, a real estate developer in the Mid-Atlantic, had asked me to come up with a wetlands plan for a new resort community. He wanted to create an education center in keeping with his devotion to environmental protection. He wanted to do more than just abide by regulations. He wanted to teach people why wetlands matter and why they must be kept pristine.

It was my first project with the company, where I had begun work a month earlier. I was looking forward to working on exciting projects in these thriving communities, and I was eager to prove my worth. I undertook hours of research and put together a plan for a visitor center at the resort, with walking trails and interactive learning.

I was certain he would be pleased with all my hard work. But he said not a word during my presentation, and he was silent afterward as well. That's not a good sign when you are dealing with a highly gregarious man.

"It seems as if you've been talking to Wilson," he finally said.

I couldn't recall meeting anyone named Wilson at the company. Josh was a movie buff, and he was referring to Tom Hanks' volleyball in *Cast Away*. In the film, Hanks' character is marooned alone on a deserted island, following an airplane crash. In the debris, he finds a Wilson-brand volleyball, draws a face on it, and begins relating to it as if it were human, engaging in one-way conversations. He names his companion Wilson.

> **It would have been okay to acknowledge that I wasn't the expert, particularly in light of the short time I had been there.**

Here's how Josh went on to explain himself:

I told you I had a vision for this property, but instead of talking to me or anyone else in the company, it sounds like you had this whole conversation in your head, in your own world. You don't have to talk to Wilson. We're all here to work with you.

It would have been okay to acknowledge that I wasn't the expert, particularly in light of the short time I had been there. He wasn't looking for what I knew, but how well I could collaborate with others. In that moment, I realized my success with the company would come from teamwork and soliciting input.

In demonstrating candor, he set the tone for open, honest, direct communication across the company. And he impressed on me the importance of engagement—that, as a group, we are collectively more success-ful than when we are working independently.

> *I was mortified at the time, but in retrospect I see that he was honest with me and wanted me to understand, early on, what success would look like in his firm.*

I am grateful to him for that, among so many other things. As one of my own lessons in candor, the experience helped shape the person and professional I have become. I was mortified at the time, but in retrospect I see that he was honest with me and wanted me to understand, early on, what success would look like in his firm.

Later, I worked for Josh as a consultant. He would have me write speeches for him, although I found it frustrating that he often ad libbed. People would tell me how good his speeches were, and I would ask, "So what was the best part?" And, usually, it was something I hadn't written.

One speech I wrote for him was for a graduation ceremony at a small college in Delaware. The local newspaper reported on how powerful his message was, and sure enough, he had gone his own way yet again. The content was entirely different. In addition, he had deter-mined that English was a second language for a large percentage of the graduates. So he delivered the entire revised address alternating between Spanish and English. This was a man who had not graduated from college himself. Remarkable.

I asked him once why I was writing speeches for him if he was going to deliver them so differently. "Nancy," he told me, "I couldn't do that without you. You start me on the path to what I will say, and I need you for that." I realized that what he wanted was for me to give him an opening. His was the highly active mind of a visionary, frequently pursuing new ideas, sometimes by the minute. He was always refining and improving. He wanted me to know that he valued me for giving him the framework within which he could do so.

Earlier, that had been the essence of his message to me when he chided me for not including others in planning the environmental center. He wanted me to contribute toward providing a framework for everyone's ideas, not to do the job alone on my island, talking only to myself.

FEEDBACK WITH GRACE

There were so many lessons in this for me. I saw the importance of soliciting the creative energy of all those around me. I learned to never assume that I knew what would be best for others without even asking them. And it was a demonstration, for me, on the importance of helping new employees get off to a good start so that they have every chance to be successful.

> *I learned to never assume that I knew what would be best for others without even asking them.*

98

A lot of times, the boss will shrug off an issue as no big deal, thinking the employee will get better in time. But just how long will that take? Those first few months are a critical stage for new employees. They form their work patterns and habits and learn what is expected of them if they are to be considered successful. Feedback during that time is critical. It's a mistake to dismiss an issue as "no big deal" when it could be a prime learning opportunity in the collegial spirit of "this is what we need, and this is how we work together." When you tell people what they need to know and do to succeed, you honor them.

And how does the employee honor the boss? By taking that feedback graciously, even if it might seem challenging. I once had a professor coach me on the importance of accepting hard feedback for what it is worth.

One day, I met with the professor and a technical expert to acquire some new skills. This expert gave me some initial, very difficult feedback on my efforts. I just listened and nodded. But it was the harshest feedback I think I have ever gotten. It took every ounce of my being to be present and to hang in.

After she left, I turned to the professor. "I have to ask you," I said, "should we continue? I don't want to spend a day if your mindset is that this will not make a difference, that the talent just isn't here and technique won't matter enough."

He said, "Actually, what I was watching was how well you could handle the feedback. Because if you had gotten defensive or pushed back, or argued, or gotten upset, then I would have wondered if we could have a good day. But you took it so well. I think we're going to have a great day." The professor was looking for whether I was open to learning. Would I be willing to hear new perspectives? He wanted to see up front whether I could adapt.

Likewise, the first 30 to 90 days for new employees are when supervisors will see how they take feedback. Will they accept the information and do things differently? It is unrealistic to presume new employees will just know what is expected. At the end of those three months, it makes little sense for supervisors to proclaim what new employees didn't do right if they were never told that those things mattered in their organization.

Just as the employee can talk to Wilson, so can the boss. If true conversation isn't happening, everyone loses out on opportunities for a better outcome. When people talk to themselves, how can they expect a genuine response?

THE PERILS OF PRESUMPTION

This principle applies not only in the office but also within families and among friends, and other relationships both professional and personal. "It matters to me," people often presume, "so it must matter to everyone." They know their own priorities, and they know how they would do things and what they must never overlook, and somehow they come to believe that everyone naturally has that same game plan.

Far better if we were to simply tell others, "To me, the most important thing is this . . . and that is what I am looking for." Instead, we presume things about people. We believe we know what is best and they have the same perceptions, and yet we have never clearly shared our own views and feelings with them. We don't tell them how to do a project, presuming they already know how to deliver good results, and they very well may be quite adept at doing so, but in a different context. They need to know specific expectations. Similarly, at work or at home, it is important to let others know how you wish to be treated. They likely have their own ideas about how people want to be treated, but each of us is unique.

Just as that lack of candor can wreak havoc in the workplace, so it can also lead to serious dysfunction elsewhere. Those silent assumptions do not encourage the healthy interactions and open discourse that we need in our homes, our communities, our government, our culture.

SPEAKING TRUTH TO POWER

Because we are so carefully taught as children how we should behave, we come to exhibit a number of beliefs as adults. Experience sometimes teaches us that we will do damage by speaking up, and that we will face consequences worse than if we just shut up. It comes down to fear.

In the workplace, we can have the fear that we will court trouble if we evaluate people candidly. What if they decide they no longer want to work for our company? Maybe they will speak ill of us during an exit interview, and then, what if we don't get promoted, and what if we don't get that raise? We worry that we might be seen as a trouble-maker or a naysayer, or the one who everyone says throws people or projects under the bus. All that just because we opened our mouths.

Those fearful responses—What if this happens? What if that happens? Maybe I'd better shut up—become ingrained in many children. They are told they should speak only when they are spoken to, or that they should temper their remarks, or they may worry that everything they say will be judged. Later, as adults, they can have difficulty dealing openly with those whom they perceive to be authority figures. People can come to anticipate a lot of bad consequences from speaking openly. Whether they are dealing with the boss or with a significant other, candor often just doesn't seem worth the risk.

> *We worry that we might be seen as a troublemaker or a naysayer, or the one who everyone says throws people or projects under the bus. All that just because we opened our mouths.*

It is important for all of us to learn to speak truth to power. Yes, we want to maintain respect. It would do us little good to snap at a police officer who is giving us a traffic ticket, for example. But let's stand up for ourselves so that situations are resolved effectively. We have a right to explain how we see matters, with due regard to the power that others might hold. In a courtroom, for example, we need to honor the judge, but we also are obligated to speak the whole truth.

When I talk about the importance of candor, however, I don't mean that we should tell everybody everything. We don't need to divulge our salary to coworkers just because they ask, for example. We probably would not want to tell our new romantic interest that we had an affair fifteen years ago. That's not necessarily candor. Some information is private or inappropriate in certain settings or contexts.

You may have seen the television commercial in which Abe Lincoln's wife, Mary, asks him whether her dress makes her backside look big. He struggles with how to answer. He's Honest Abe, after all. Finally, he concedes that perhaps it does, a bit. You can imagine the consequences.

> When I talk about the importance of candor, however, I don't mean that we should tell everybody everything.

By and large, however, when people ask you for an opinion about something, they want a sincere answer, and they generally deserve one. Unless you encourage that spirit of openness, they might cease to seek your viewpoints on anything. The key is to find a way to answer questions so that you are honest with yourself and with others and don't run them down with criticism. You can do harm by saying things that don't need to be said and, as Honest Abe found out, it's a fine line. We learn where to draw that line through practice, maturity, and experience.

FACING UP TO FEARS

Often the reason that people hesitate to speak with candor is that they fear how others will react. They may find that taking that risk is well worth it. The photographer Platon learned that during an encounter with actor Anthony Hopkins.

Platon has photographed more than 120 heads of state for *Rolling Stone*, the *New York Times Magazine*, *Vanity Fair*, *Esquire*, and *GQ*. His iconic shots of such notables as Vladimir Putin, Muammar Al-Gaddafi, and Bill Clinton draw immediate global recognition and appreciation. Yet, he related to a Richmond Forum audience how frightened he was capturing Hopkins on film.

It was one of Platon's first assignments and he was sent to photograph Hopkins, who later won the Academy Award for his portrayal of the cannibalistic villain Hannibal Lector in the movie *Silence of the Lambs.*

As Platon tells the story: "I was preparing the night before for my scheduled sitting with Anthony Hopkins. I was watching TV and heard on the news that Sir Anthony had beaten up the *Vogue* photographer who was sent to capture his image on film earlier that day."

Platon felt that did not bode well for his own assignment with Hopkins. He was nervous as he set up his equipment the following day at the appointed time.

Mr. Hopkins arrived and we did our introductions and began to set to work. I suddenly felt very nauseous, my legs and arms were shaking and I felt terrible. I truly thought I was having a heart attack, but I later discovered that it was a panic attack. I didn't know what to do. I thought I might pass out at any moment. I said, "I'll be honest with you. I am not a photographer. I am an art student and you are my first job like this. And I am worried that I will be beat up like the Vogue photographer was yesterday." Mr. Hopkins then asked, "Listen, did it not occur to you that I'm scared too? I hate to have my picture taken." Then he remarked, "You have been honest with me and I appreciate it. We will make a picture together."

Platon reported they then had a very successful engagement. This is another example of when candor promotes connection and can defuse tension, even when it involves one of the best-known movie serial killers of all time.

Platon decided to stop talking to Wilson. He went right to the source, and even though he no doubt felt it was a risk to even suggest the prospect of Hopkins hitting him, his panic attack immediately abated. That's the power of candor: Even in moments of high stress, it can connect people. It allows them to share their humanity. In this case, the truth of the matter was that each was harboring a fear. Platon found out what was going through Hopkins' head, rather than just imagining what he might do.

> *That's the power of candor: Even in moments of high stress, it can connect people. It allows them to share their humanity.*

DOES ANYBODY CARE?

We might also hold back from communicating clearly with others because we suspect that they don't really care what we have to say. We figure their minds are made up, so why try? Sometimes, it's true that people can be quite firm in their beliefs, but you really don't know until you talk with them. If nobody bothered to do so, we would be sorely lacking in the open debate that is the linchpin of our political system.

I experienced firsthand the importance of such clarity when the chamber of commerce invited members of our Virginia legislature to a dinner. I wanted to talk, in particular, about a major transportation initiative that was important to the entire business community.

During the dinner, I talked privately to one of the legislators, who sat to my right. We couldn't have seen the world more differently. I tried to convince him that our initiative really mattered, but he was resistant. I finally asked, "Is there anything about this bill that you could find appealing? Or anything that we could do with it so that you would find yourself able to vote for it?"

"I will never vote for it in any form," he said, "because if I do, I will not be reelected in my community." I appreciated knowing that. He gave me his truth. I could have lobbied him forever to no avail, because that was how he decided matters. His candor allowed me to turn left for a more fruitful conversation.

He had identified his sticking point. He was not interested in talking about the components of the bill. He was focused on keeping his job. Because he was that forthright with me, I was able to move on and use my time wisely. His candor had shown me just what I was dealing with.

It did indeed seem to me that he didn't really care what I had to say, but I said it anyway, and he was remarkably clear, for a politician, about his motivations. He was going to vote for what would please his voting constituency. Knowing that, I thought perhaps somebody other than I, someone with more experience at persuading politicians, could make a pitch to him on how the legislation would help him at the polls.

JUST WHOM ARE WE PROTECTING?

Sometimes, people are not frank because they feel that they need to protect others from bad news. Under the surface, however, they may also be thinking this: "I also don't want to tell them this bad news, because it may reflect badly on me."

> *Sometimes, people are not frank because they feel that they need to protect others from bad news.*

The controversy over the death of Pat Tillman, an Army Ranger killed in Afghanistan, illustrates that misguided stance. His widow, Marie Tillman, has written about what happened in her book *The Letter*. She says that certain members of the U.S. Army were not forthright about how her husband died and describes the tremendous impact it had on her and others in the family.

Tillman, who played for the Arizona Cardinals from 1998 through 2001, was among the many who reassessed their lives after the 9/11 terrorist attacks. He turned down a three-year, $3.6 million contract offer from the Cardinals and enlisted in the Army in May 2002.

Marie explained (in a 2012 interview with CNN's Piers Morgan) that Pat, "took a step back and reprioritized what was important to him in his life . . . He really felt called to serve his country." Pat served first in Iraq, returned stateside to train as an Army Ranger and was redeployed to Afghanistan, where he was killed in action in April 2004.

Marie says she and her family were first told that he was killed in an enemy ambush. The subsequent autopsy and additional conflicting details surrounding his death triggered an investigation. The investigation not only concluded that Pat was killed by friendly fire (inadvertently by his own men while engaged in enemy action), but that many of the involved Army personnel also took actions to cover up the real cause of his death.

While his wife's story of Tillman's life and death has so many interesting elements, I was struck by her descriptions about what this lack of candor and the accompanying cover-up meant to her.

Since learning the truth, here is what she has written and spoken about in terms of the effect on her grieving process:

> When Pat and Kevin (his brother) enlisted, we had felt unified as a family, but also felt we were part of a much bigger military family. We were all in this together. That's why our treatment after his death felt like such a betrayal. And the thing is, once you've been lied to, you start to think no one's telling the truth. Conspiracy theories about Pat's death started to circulate . . . If he'd died some other way, this changed everything. If what they had told me at first was wrong, maybe the whole thing was wrong. Maybe he was still alive. I do think that the families of the soldiers that are serving deserve to know the truth about their deaths. I think that's something that's just a common decency.

What happens when what we think people may be ready to hear, or what we are comfortable saying clashes with "the real deal"? Does this inform us about delivering devastating news to people? How do we continue to honor people with full candor when the going gets very tough?

Whether it was to protect the family or to avoid embarrassment, the military was not forthright with Tillman's family about how he died.

Whatever the reason for hiding the truth, the consequence was that the family had to grieve twice. When hearts are ripped open again, they have to heal again, and once you lie to people, they become skeptical and may start to think no one is telling them the truth.

> *Whatever the reason for hiding the truth, the consequence was that the family had to grieve twice.*

Such was the cost of the lack of candor. That family felt betrayed, not protected. When we decree that people can't handle things or that we know what will be better for them, do we have the right to make such a decision?

ECHOES OF CHILDHOOD

Such a paternal stance might be more fitting when directed at a child, but even then, it's a fine line. Young people eventually realize when the adults are feeding them untruths regularly in a misguided effort to protect them. Some people go through life carrying the emotional burden of such mistreatment.

The echoes of childhood can reverberate throughout a lifetime. Unless people come to terms with those memories, they might mistrust others in general and lack candor in relationships, and so the cycle continues, generation to generation. But even if others have not trusted us with the truth in the past, we can learn to trust that others will be able to handle it.

We can learn, also, that speaking one's mind does not make one unlikable. We need not abide by a childhood perception that we must be agreeable at all costs—and those costs can be quite high. The friend that we feared losing might turn out to be no friend at all.

> *We need not abide by a childhood perception that we must be agreeable at all costs—and those costs can be quite high.*

People have often told me that they feel conflicted about giving feedback, because a friend or workplace colleague might like them less. It's a fear that keeps relationships, both business and personal, from being anything more than shallow.

"Be nice" is the message, repeated to the point where it can become the cultural norm. I've heard it called "the Southern way" and "Minnesota nice," and I've heard women disparagingly called "Stepford wives," a reference to a novel and movie about a New England town's docile darlings.

When we choose to live solely by others' expectations, we are not all that different from those *Stepford Wives* robots. We are not being real, and we are not being true to ourselves. We are just reflecting somebody else's vision of niceness. We feel that the way to maintain relationships is to keep on smiling and to keep conversations at a surface level.

People who are like that, in our family, at work, or in the community, end up being rather ineffectual. Little do they know that candor is what builds respect and that direct talk is what deepens relationships.

Yes, everyone indeed may consider them to be quite agreeable folks, but do they get the tough assignments that require people skills and negotiation? How many CEOs got to their position by just smiling and nodding and shaking hands? And in public life, how many politicians— all jokes aside—ever make it to high office without exhibiting some depth of personality?

> *They adopt the attitude that it is better to be silent than to be wrong.*

There's a significant difference between being liked and being respected. Which are you looking for? Sometimes we don't turn that corner until we're more seasoned in our careers. To be respected actually carries a higher value in many people's minds than to be liked. Most people can think of a U.S. president or corporate executive whom they liked but did not respect as a great leader, and most also can think of one who they concede was a great leader even though they did not much like him or her. Often, candor is so honoring of others that it can garner both respect and likeability.

THE SILENCE OF INSECURITY

"What if I'm wrong?" is another reason that people hold back from expressing themselves openly and honestly. They lack candor because of an insecure fear they will appear inept or weak if they reveal that their understanding of something is incorrect. They adopt the attitude that it is better to be silent than to be wrong.

Much of the time, it is not a matter of whether we are right or wrong, but, rather, it is a matter of expressing our opinions, and again we need to remember that someone who asks for that opinion generally values it and wants to hear it straight, Mrs. Lincoln notwithstanding.

I once visited a dress shop with several friends, and one of them emerged from the dressing room and asked, with a smile, "So what do you think of this?" I looked around, and, unfortunately, I was the only one of our group who was nearby. She looked at me. "Well, Nancy?"

She was wearing a large, white overblouse. In my opinion, it was not flattering. I thought, "Okay, if it's me she is asking, then I've simply got to tell her."

"I think it makes you look larger than you are," I said, bracing myself.

"But it's really comfortable," she said.

"Well, if you like it, buy it," I said, and she did.

And today, when she wears it, she tells people, "Nancy didn't like this, but I bought it anyway."

And I remind her, "Now wait, I didn't say I didn't like it. You asked me for my opinion about it, and I gave you my opinion about it."

She reserves that blouse for those occasions when comfort trumps looks. But the question she posed to me concerned how it looked, and I was true to a friend. We laugh about it every time.

A little good humor goes a long way toward keeping a relationship running smoothly, whether between friends or colleagues. You cannot really argue with an opinion. It's neither right nor wrong. You can be mistaken about a fact, of course, and a procedure can be correct or incorrect, but unless you are doing brain surgery or designing a rocket ship, consider that, in many instances, it just might be okay to be wrong. You won't have all the answers. What is important is to be open and be part of the conversation.

KNOWING WHAT WE DON'T KNOW

Think of it this way: Do you think the president of a hospital is the best at heart transplants? Is it likely that the owner of a football team would make a good quarterback? Is the CEO of a bank always the best lender?

Good leaders delegate. They know what they don't know, or where others have the needed expertise, and they surround themselves with the right people. They don't try to fake it, as if they were the masters of all trades. They admit it when they are uncertain or lack information and are looking for advice and direction. They often preface their statements like this: "I may be wrong, but it seems to me . . ."

You may recall Ed Harris's portrayal of Gene Kranz, the flight director for the troubled moon mission in the movie *Apollo 13*. "Failure is not an option," he declares, rallying the team at Mission Control. He was a leader, not a technician. He had to keep trusting people and making decisions based on the information that the engineers were bringing him, and there was a lot at stake.

The average age of those engineers was 26. While not much older, the flight director had something they lacked, which was leadership experience and a developed ability to synthesize and prioritize all of that information. The right decisions depend on a lot more than calculations and schematics. There's a reason that the founders of our nation decided a presidential candidate needs to be at least 35 years old. That age offers at least some reassurance of experience in dealing with people. Truly accomplished leaders know what they don't know and delegate duties so that they can focus on what they do best—that is, leadership.

> *Truly accomplished leaders know what they don't know and delegate duties so that they can focus on what they do best—that is, leadership.*

GIFTS FROM THE HEAD AND THE HEART

I think back to Josh, my boss at the real estate development company who suggested that I stop talking to Wilson. He was a true mentor to me and probably had as much of an influence as anyone on how I viewed being effective, how I viewed giving feedback, and how I progressed in my career and personally. I was older than he was—he was 42—but he had already shared a wealth of lessons with me.

Josh will never be older than 42.

When he passed away tragically, as a result of a helicopter crash, it left a void for hundreds and hundreds of people whose lives he had touched.

He taught me so much in our eight years together, five as an employee and three as a consultant. He had an everlasting influence on my life and on the lives of many others. He gave of his head, and he gave of his heart.

CHAPTER 7

THE DIRECT APPROACH

"When you want something, start with the direct approach. That is, go straight to the source and ask for what you want. You will be surprised at how often you get it."
—JOHN T. REED

IF YOU HAD A MAGIC WAND and could wave it and change three things in your company immediately, what would they be? It's a question that I ask clients early in our relationship. Often, when I am called in to work with an organization, I find people who are feeling some level of distress about things that aren't going the way they wish. They are transitioning, or they're doing something they have not done before, or an important business relationship isn't working well. They have decided they need somebody to coach them to a breakthrough.

Invariably, what I hear from either boards or CEOs is something like this: "I wish people would tell me the truth."

They wish that when they ask people questions, they would actually get the facts. They want to be able to count on what they are hearing, without any spin or cover-up. They don't want to hear Pollyannas who say everything is going to be just fine—until it's not. They aren't interested in comments merely aimed at protecting somebody's job, and they are weary of the attitude that the CEO, or the board chair, doesn't really need or want to hear the truth.

IN SEARCH OF THE REAL DEAL

When I speak with people about what they want from their leaders, I often hear that they want to know where they stand; they want to hear about what really matters; and they want to be direct but don't feel free to do so. They say, "I don't think he wants to hear the real deal about what's going on." Such comments tell me that something's not working, and perhaps it's a matter of feeling comfortable and safe enough to bring up that real deal.

> *They don't want to hear Pollyannas who say everything is going to be just fine—until it's not.*

What strikes me is everybody says they want the truth, and yet, whether it's our human nature or things we have set up in our organizations, we don't feel we are getting that truth. We are operating in a culture in which most people say they want something different, but it doesn't happen often.

What, then, will encourage more candor? What will lead coworkers and family members alike to bring essential matters out into the open so they can deal with them? If you feel people need some correction, you're hardly encouraging them by saying you believe they are doing just fine. Addressing the issue is the most encouraging thing you can do. You are offering an opportunity for change.

Consider that your silence can be cruel if it allows someone to sink deeper into peril. It happens to bosses who are afraid to engage in real managing. It happens to mothers and fathers who are afraid to engage in real parenting. It happens to friends who are acting more like casual acquaintances.

This is not to suggest that your observations should have a judgmental tone to them. One can be straightforward without going on the offensive. It's helpful to practice talking about issues in terms of the facts, and the fact of the matter may be that someone is not delivering the needed results.

> *It's helpful to practice talking about issues in terms of the facts, and the fact of the matter may be that someone is not delivering the needed results.*

So why not start there? Say something like, "The results we expect are this, and we're not getting them, so how are we going to change that?" That's the kind of clarification that motivates. It is important to stay with the facts and not embellish them with your own feelings. That's not candor. That's trouble.

Candor requires care. People who feel they have been wronged can go on creative flights of imagination about the perceived perpetrator, whereas, in truth, they are not seeing what they think they are seeing. If someone has his arms crossed while talking to you, does it mean he is blocking you off or taking an aggressive stance, or does it mean he is a little chilly? Remember, you can always ask, "Your arms are crossed. What does that mean?" Instead of talking to Wilson about it, you can go right to the source and give people a chance to tell you what they think and feel.

DEALING WITH THE OBNOXIOUS UNCLE

Like everything, it starts with first steps. Think about that nasty uncle. There seems to be someone like him in most families, if the newspaper advice columns are to be believed, someone who is invited with reluctance for Thanksgiving dinner. He's loud and offensive, possibly drunk, and appears to do his best to ruin the day. Families seem to go to great lengths to accommodate people like that. They will find any number of things to say to him or ways to invite him that keep him away from the family for all but a brief time. They try a lot of creative workarounds so that he doesn't wreck the holiday. Meanwhile, the nasty uncle is at the center of all this fuss, and that may be just what he wants. It's working for him.

> *It's far better to directly deal with that person at a time that you choose, not when the problem is at hand.*

Why not just refuse to put up with it? Try something different. Consider telling him that he needs to change, or it's over. "Here's what we require of you this year. If you think you can abide by that, you are welcome to come. If you can't, please do not come." That's a conversation people avoid having. They do not address people like that, people who continue to be a drain on time and energy as they throw others into a frenzy to accommodate them.

It's far better to directly deal with that person at a time that you choose, not when the problem is at hand. That is honoring. The offender gets the message clearly and others don't spend time muttering about him when he hasn't yet been told that he's out of line.

Children need to be told when they are misbehaving. Otherwise, they won't know. Sometimes, as adults, we need to be told when we're misbehaving; that way, we have a chance to do something about it. It's not confrontational. It's constructive. It's building for something better rather than capitulating to what is broken.

Similar situations occur in the workplace. If somebody is not delivering, or the results aren't happening, or the relationships are broken, the same kind of workaround happens. Others avoid that person. They don't invite him or her to be involved in projects. The person who is not delivering almost becomes a pariah in the organization. Others don't want to be associated with such poor work.

Some workarounds can be more subtle but just as damaging. Let's say I'm a boss and I have an employee who gives me a report to review, and I think he or she has missed the mark. But let's say I just fix the problem and send the report on. As a result, the employee may never learn to do it correctly and continues to do B-level work, assuming I will just change it anyway. Not having been told, such employees cannot improve, and I end up with still more of somebody else's work to do myself. This is counterproductive to getting velocity and results in an organization.

DEALING DIRECTLY

In our practice, we use a "DIRECT" communication guide that helps to ensure productive conversations on performance feedback and effective interaction in challenging situations. In the early days of Pathwise Partners, Jeannie Shaughnessy and I developed this tool.

Each of the letters of the word DIRECT stands for a step in this method of effective communication, which, in essence, calls for dealing directly with others in a manner that encourages candor.

Here are the steps to that guide, as we present them to our clients: *(See chart on page 123).*

Determine your objectives and desired outcomes (and roles for participation) for the communication/conversation. Also determine the best venue/location.

Setting objectives is the most crucial step in this process: What do you want to happen as a result of this conversation? Is it a specific action? Is it understanding more about the situation? Do you wish to explore new opportunities for success? Are you interested in improving the relationship?

Often, there are multiple objectives. For example, you may want to clarify and learn more about a situation. You may want to learn another's perspective. You may want to come to an aligned agreement on next steps while ensuring an improved working relationship. Determining all these up front increases the chances of a successful outcome.

Note: Sometimes, the real objective or set of objectives feels like too much, is too big, or too scary to approach in one com-

Determine your objectives and desired outcomes (and roles for participation) for the communication/conversation. Also determine the best venue/location.	1. Objectives: 2. Desired Outcomes: 3. Best Location/Venue: 4. Expectations (listen/decision/solution):
Introduce context and the purpose of the communication/feedback from your perspective – along with any anxieties/fears you may have.	1. Context: 2. Purpose: 3. Anxieties/Fears:
Remember to focus on the facts involved in the situation, remove the "wrong" from the conversation and consider "their world." Be free of assumptions when you enter the conversation.	1. Facts: 2. Assumptions you have made (to dismiss prior):
Engage the participant and ask what they have heard from you (remember the level of listening likely to occur). Resist the temptation to "predict" how the conversation will go.	1. Determine key points in the conversation to "check-in":
Consider your relationship with those in the conversation – and speak in the context of your commitment to their development and their (your collective) success.	1. Consider your relationship: 2. State your commitment to:
Take the time to provide feedback – and remember, important conversations typically don't take as much time as you might imagine. Be prepared to "hang" in the conversation until you are satisfied that the communication is complete and that your objectives have been met. We often leave a little too early...and then need to return to the difficult (incomplete) conversation.	1. Determine/set the time: 2. Identify what's required for you to be complete:

munication. Unless time constraints forbid it, sometimes biting off a bit at a time gives access to the first and easiest conversation. The first conversation could just be a sharing of perspectives about a situation that needs improvement. Then you can schedule the next conversation to meet the next likely/appropriate objective.

Introduce the context and the purpose of the communication or feedback from your perspective, along with any anxieties and fears you might have.

This is a great way to set the foundation for the communication. Describe the purpose of this communication and why it matters to me, you, or the organization. Explain why you are initiating this communication. Define your hopes or worries for this conversation.

In sharing these, you are giving context, bringing others along your journey of preparation, and sharing any fears or vulnerabilities you may have. It often draws similar sharing of fears or anxieties from others, paving the way for a meaty conversation.

Remember to focus on the facts involved in the situation, remove the "wrong" from the conversation and consider "their world." Be free of assumptions when you enter the conversation.

State the facts, free of blame and challenge. For example, "I want to review yesterday's client presentation, to focus on what we wish had done better in that presentation, and how we will continually improve for the next time." Or, "This morning we discussed a tense topic and others told me they could hear our raised voices." Or, "Your draft presentation was due this morning and I don't see it."

Keep all assumptions at bay. We often don't know the "why." Assumptions are like talking to Wilson.

Engage the participants and ask what they have heard from you (remember the level of listening likely to occur). Resist the temptation to "predict" how the conversation will go.

Questions about what they have heard from you, what it makes them think about, and what questions they have of you are all good ways to know whether your intent matches your impact. Did your message land as you had hoped? Did your partner in the conversation hear the key message?

Encourage each person's involvement at each of these steps. Good questions are: Does that match with your view of the incident? What are your recommendations for improvement? How can we best avoid that situation in the future? Who else do we need to collaborate with, or partner with, to solve this? What do you wish you had done differently? What would you not change for the next time?

Consider your relationship with those in the conversation, and speak in the context of your commitment to their development and your collective success.

If you are speaking with someone with whom you have an excellent relationship, and to whom you feel you could say almost anything, consider mentioning that, if it is a reason you are communicating so candidly. If your relationship is new or rocky, that might also be worth a mention. It is a nice way to break the ice: "I know we have just started working together, so I was hoping this conversation would grow our relationship." And if you add, "I am committed to a great outcome for you, me, the company, and the client in this discussion," you will be making your intent very clear.

Take the time to provide feedback, and remember important conversations typically don't take as much time as you might imagine. Be prepared to stay with the conversation until you are satisfied that the communication is complete and that your objectives have been met. We often leave a little too early and then need to return to the difficult conversation that wasn't completed.

Often, we address one part of the conversation and it goes exceedingly well, or just the opposite. And our time pressures and human sense of relief at getting it behind us cause us to close the conversation to avoid more discomfort. When you have the door open on how to improve results and relationships, it is a good time to ask if anything else has not been said or discussed that would be helpful.

THE CULTURE COMES FROM THE TOP

At all levels, we want the same thing, and until we take the initiative to be more direct and forthright, others around us will not be that way.

The culture comes from the top. It's a trickle-down effect. The leadership establishes the culture, and when people see what acceptable leadership is, or what preferred behavior is, they tend to adopt it.

Until the CEO or others put the emphasis on candor, it isn't likely to permeate the organization. If, for example, the leaders don't seem to care about celebrating and instead just issue critiques about what was done wrong, then the entire staff gets the impression that celebrating accomplishment and success is not what leaders do there. Eventually, people may not aspire to higher positions in the company and will look elsewhere for career satisfaction.

> *The leadership establishes the culture, and when people see what acceptable leadership is, or what preferred behavior is, they tend to adopt it.*

A bleak culture can kill business. Whether it is intentional or not, that's no small consequence of neglect from the top. The prescription to cure this blight is the direct and forthright approach. It's what all employees say they want, and it is proven to enhance the bottom line. If you are a leader who cares, why would you not insist on it?

CHAPTER 8

WHAT WILL IT TAKE?

"Candor ends paranoia."
—ALLEN GINSBERG

"**NANCY IS VERY GOOD** with those she thinks should be included and whose opinions matter. She needs to learn more from people she disagrees with." I was mortified to read those words, and it would not be the last time that I felt that way just before learning a life lesson.

I was in graduate school at the time, and I had a job with the university that paid for my education. I worked for the chairman of the Psychology department, a very wise man. I needed a reference for something I was applying for. Whether it was a fellowship or a job, I can't recall, but what I do remember so vividly is how he responded.

I took a form in and asked him if he would fill it out as my reference, and Dr. Ray Kirby said to me, "I will, but I'm also going to give you a copy of it." At that time, for students to get a copy of their reference letter wasn't usual. You just asked somebody for a reference that you would never actually see.

So he gave me the copy of the completed reference form, and on it were the typical questions: What do you see as this applicant's weaknesses? Where does this applicant need to show improvement?

After I composed myself, I went to his office to talk about his answer. "Really?" I asked.

"Really," he said.

I reflected a moment and then told him that I understood what he was saying. "You're right," I said. "I mean, I know I do this. But why?"

"Whatever the reason," he said, "what's important is to just always remember that you can learn from everybody, including those who you think are wrong. You should listen to what those people have to say, too."

This was a man who was critical to my success. He was not only my boss, but he also headed the department from which I was getting my degree. He cared far more about whether I understood that lesson than about whether his reference helped me land my prize. He wasn't worried that I might not like him anymore if he didn't write a glowing endorsement.

He felt no intimidation, just a clear opportunity to be perfectly candid. He was the ultimate mentor and teacher, and he valued clarity. I could see that in how he handled my request. He wrote it out and made sure I had time to think about it before returning to see him. He knew that would promote my most thoughtful response. He didn't let me miss this opportunity to improve, in the true spirit of education.

I have spent the years since then on the path to that improvement, and I know today that I deeply value the kind of inclusive conversation that solicits all viewpoints. We all would be well advised to work harder at including the perspectives of those with whom we disagree. That's what makes a well-rounded personality, a stronger and more productive business culture, a more-diverse, less-cynical, and unbiased society. If we do not encourage the free exchange of opinions, then our relationships stagnate, as do any institutions based on them, which is to say, all of them.

> *We all would be well advised to work harder at including the perspectives of those with whom we disagree.*

"WHAT IF YOU WERE TO ACTUALLY SAY THAT?"

Today, I am in the business of promoting clarification and reducing confrontation and concession. I am an advocate of candor in communication so that everyone involved understands one another's positions and can make the best decisions.

Often, I'm called in to a company during a time of a major transition or crisis. Perhaps there has been an acquisition, or a new product or service has been introduced into the marketplace. Perhaps a major client has been lost, or a competitor is taking all the business, or there's no longer a market for the product. Maybe a key executive has acted badly and is about to be released from the company.

The CEO or the board chair or someone will say, "We have this crisis and we need to talk to stakeholders, investors, shareholders, the public, customers, employees, about it." When the executive starts to tell me about the situation, I can already hear the layers of spin on it.

Whether corporate America is dealing with product recalls, data breaches by hackers, or food-borne illnesses, we still don't do it well.

It comes out as very genteel, and very unclear, and I am asked, "Does that make sense? Is that how we should talk about it? What should we do? How do we take care of this? How do we fix it, and then how do we talk about it?"

Often, what I will say is, "Suppose it's just you and me, and you could just tell me every single fact about it. What would you say?" That's when the executive lays it out for me, telling me just how it is, from beginning to end, the good, the bad, and the ugly of the situation.

"Well," I say, "what if you were to actually say that?"

You can almost see the tension leave the executive's body, just at the thought of doing that. "I would love to!" he or she says, and then adds, "But I can't."

The reason might be that human resources, or the public relations folks, or the lawyers who protect the company from litigation have forbidden that approach. Or there is a fear that the stock price will drop. And those are all legitimate, appropriate concerns. We work from there: "Well, let's see what we can do that helps to mitigate those risks, coming from a place that's so authentic that people get it."

Regrettably, we often have to go back to the Johnson & Johnson situation of long ago to find good examples of candid crisis communications. Whether corporate America is dealing with product recalls, data breaches by hackers, or food-borne illnesses, we still don't do it well.

CANDOR MEANS SURVIVAL

Companies should recognize that candor is essential to their survival. The truth must be out. Yes, executives in crisis will worry about all the collateral damage, but open conversation is the first step in reframing the situation and realizing how very honoring such candor is to all involved. "But people won't believe us" is the excuse often offered. It is true that if you are *not* being forthright, people won't believe you. They are smarter than some executives might think, and they remember.

> *It is true that if you are not being forthright, people won't believe you. They are smarter than some executives might think, and they remember.*

Candor might be painful in the moment, but what feels uncomfortable now is likely to promote far more comfort ahead. There is a cleanness that comes from telling the truth. You don't have to worry about what you said before. You don't have to keep saying words that aren't authentically yours, words that a lawyer or public relations professional devised in the well-intentioned belief that the proper statement may avoid litigation or sound better. Heed their advice and then speak in your own words.

I ask people, "Is there a time when somebody in your life told you the truth and you later appreciated it, even though it made everybody uncomfortable in the moment?" They always have a story to relate to me. And so the next question is, "So why would you not allow others to have that great experience?"

Even if they don't ask for it, if you feel that it's essential information, speak up. It can be life changing, or corporation changing, or community changing.

CHALLENGE GREATER THAN EVER

For generations, the business world has not much diversity of thought. People have become accustomed to associating with fellow employees who share the same perspectives and often have much the same background.

> *The only way to find out what people of other cultures and backgrounds and demographics are thinking is to ask them and be a good listener.*

Our world and our workplaces have become more diverse, more global. We may want to understand our coworkers and how to interact with them effectively, but often we are not successful. It requires a learning curve, and it can be a particularly steep one for somebody in a new position with a new level of authority. It is not surprising that people encounter difficulties doing things that they have never done before, with people they have never done them with before, who may see the world differently.

The only way to find out what people of other cultures and backgrounds and demographics are thinking is to ask them and be a good listener. We need to constantly seek clarification and keep the conversation continuous, with a stream of observations and inquiries: Here's where I want to go. Here's what I see. What do you see? How do we do this together? What's in the way? Those questions do not assume that we know best, because we only know what we know. A lot of people in their careers have been very successful based on what they know, and when people get to real leadership areas, they will be better for how well they include other people's perspectives and get to their truths about what matters. Several mentors drove that point home for me.

> *I love the fact that honesty and honor start with the same syllable.*

People often tell me that they cannot get a colleague to do something, or they point to someone with whom they have been unable to deal successfully. Communication has broken down, and that's when hope fades. Clarifying, candid conversation that gets to the heart of the matter is a way to break through that.

"LET THE PEOPLE KNOW THE FACTS"

I love the fact that honesty and honor start with the same syllable. To me, that is a reminder that they are related. When you are honest with people, you honor them. You show them the respect they deserve as thinking, feeling, creative souls. You give them the unadulterated facts they need to make intelligent decisions. You do not hide the truth from people; you give it to them straight.

The foundation of our political system is the belief that people are competent to govern themselves. When we have the facts, when we know the truth, we will make the decisions that are best for ourselves. We do not need others to decide with an iron fist what is best for us. In an open system of government, the truth will surface and the citizens will handle it well.

> *If candor has the power to save a nation, you can count on it to work wonders for you.*

That, at least, is how it works in theory. Ours is a system based on candor. Yes, our leaders fall short of candor on many occasions, but the fact that those shortcomings are broadcast far and wide is yet another indicator of the openness we value highly.

We have an obligation as citizens, as colleagues, as neighbors, as relatives, as friends to do what we can to bring the truth to others. We must make sure the facts are known, confident that when that information is brought to light, good things will happen. We must not dwell in the dark; there's such a world to see.

"Let the people know the facts, and the country will be safe." Those words of Abraham Lincoln are etched into a concrete wall at the Newseum in Washington, DC. As the president who presided over our nation's greatest crisis, he had a clear perspective on the importance of powerful leadership.

"I am a firm believer in the people," Lincoln said. "If given the truth, they can be depended upon to meet any national crisis. The great point is to bring them the real facts."

If candor has the power to save a nation, you can count on it to work wonders for you. By dedicating yourself to candor and straight talk in your workplace and in all your relationships, both professional and personal, you will open the way to greater success.

TRUE TO SELF

"Rather than love, than money,
than fame, give me truth."
—HENRY DAVID THOREAU.

I WAS ABOUT TO MEET SUPERMAN, face to face, with thousands of people watching, and what would I say?

This was the predicament I faced one evening when I was moderator for a speaker series that the bank sponsored. One of my duties at the bank was to help grow the business by building market share and adding customers. In the Washington, DC, area, however, it's very hard to get your company noticed, because media is very expensive. We also liked to do good in the community, so we came up with a few strategies that garnered brand awareness, and also brought our charitable work to bear. One was the speaker series.

We held the speakers series at George Mason University. We had identified the women-owned business segment as underserved in the 1990s, so we focused on the many important women we could host. Speakers included Katie Couric, Margaret Thatcher, Toni Morrison, and Maya Angelou.

Candice Bergen was scheduled to speak, but her husband, Louis Malle, had passed away the year before. She reached out to us and asked if there was any way she could delay her visit. We certainly understood.

At the time, Christopher Reeve, the actor well known for his portrayal of Superman, was coming to speak to Congress. This was not long after the 1995 equestrian accident that left him a quadriplegic. He was going to be in Washington, and we had the opportunity to schedule him for one of his first public appearances after his accident.

As the moderator for this series, which often included a brief Q&A session, I felt it very important that I know all the right answers and be in control, and though people reassured me, I kept coming back to that.

The husband of my best friend in graduate school was a quadriplegic, so I felt fairly comfortable about interacting with Reeve. But when he arrived, he was on a ventilator, and he had an assistant and nurse with him. His ventilator had stopped working the day before, and I was told that the nurse was there in case it happened again.

I had gotten used to the idea of speaking in front of the 2,000 people who would come to hear Reeve. I was okay with the fact that 200 of them would be our top customers. But this was something new. And Reeve had chosen to do the whole affair as Q&A, so I would be actively participating on stage with him for a full hour and a half.

I peppered his aide with nervous questions: "What if he's using the ventilator and I don't know whether he's finished his answer or just taking a deep breath? How will I know? Is there a way he can signal me? I don't want to step on his answer or cut him off before he's done."

You don't want to mess with Superman.

I was in awe of the fact that Reeve would take the time to be with us. There would be reporters and cameras everywhere because of him. I felt fraught with concerns, because I was making it all about me.

Finally, his assistant put his hand on my arm, and said, "Nancy, he has been an actor his entire life. He will own the stage."

> *I realized, again, that what I'm really good at is not being the expert.*

I just said, "Thank you." And I was able to let it all go. I realized, again, that what I'm really good at is not being the expert. I'm good at asking questions so that people can explore things for themselves and for others. I need not be the one in control. In fact, if I'm not, it's best for everybody. Reeve was the one who was going to make it all work, regardless of the situation. If I were to falter, Reeve would be there for me. He would know what to say.

I know I can ask the right questions that will lead others to greater success. It's what coaching is all about. People then find their way because they, after all, are the ones who are good at what they do. It's not about me being good at what they do.

That was an epiphany for me, though many experiences had been pointing me that way and teaching me that I probably wasn't ever the smartest one in the room and certainly not smartest in someone else's area of expertise.

I support people on their journey. I know how to probe for what really matters to them, and what's in their way. I provide a safe place to share, to be candid, to generate new possibilities, to find their own truth without anybody else there who will judge, critique, or have another agenda. They can see where they need to go and the barriers they need to move. That helps them to be true to themselves. And I have found that in helping them on that journey, I am being true to myself.

OUT IN THE OPEN

The NBA's Jason Collins is a prime example of a man who has learned to be true to himself. He made headlines by becoming the first professional male athlete in a major sport to publicly announce that he is gay.

"I'm a 34-year-old NBA center. I'm black. And I'm gay."

That's brave. That's *candor.* Collins' announcement created big waves. What's big here is not that Collins plays for the NBA, and it's not that he's gay. What *is* big is that he was publicly open and honest about an aspect of himself that could be misunderstood or could make him vulnerable.

His story does remind us, though, that candor is rarely easy. It sometimes requires us to be brave, especially if we're trekking into uncharted territory. Often, we take a deep breath, hope for the best, but, unfortunately, expect the worst. In Collins' case, his candor was praised by many, from his NBA peers to the U.S. president.

"Jason has been a widely respected player and teammate throughout his career, and we are proud he has assumed the leadership mantle on this very important issue," said David Stern, the NBA commissioner at the time.

Not everyone who chooses candor gets the same reception. How much more truthful would we be if we had confidence that we would be supported and well received? How much good could we do if candor were widely accepted? A lot, according to Collins: "Openness may not completely disarm prejudice, but it's a good place to start."

> *How much more truthful would we be if we had confidence that we would be supported and well received?*

Collins' candor came with deep meaning for our youth, future athletes, and society in general. He took a very public stand, connecting his candid actions with his happiness.

"Things can change in an instant, so why not live truthfully?" he said. "I hope that every player makes a decision that leads to their own happiness, whatever happiness that is, in life. I know that I, right now, am the happiest that I've ever been in my life."

When you are being candid and forthright, you are not necessarily only serving others. You may well be serving yourself. You are no longer living a lie.

> *What needs to be said is not always popular. But the moment of speaking up can also be the moment when healing begins, for the individual, for the organization, and for society.*

Jason Collins discovered that in his candor, he became a role model, a pacesetter. In being true to himself, he became a better person and an inspiration for others. A lot of people carry burdens around with them, holding them inside, because they decide that is less risky than letting them go and sharing them.

The truth sometimes does bring a backlash. What needs to be said is not always popular. But the moment of speaking up can also be the moment when healing begins, for the individual, for the organization, and for society.

ARROWS IN THE QUIVER

We all face obstacles. We all have times when we're not our best selves, and sometimes we carry a lot of angst about it. At times, it's not much fun. In searching for new perspectives and possibilities, we often try to overcome obstacles in the same way we have long done things. We repeat what seemed to work for us.

The trouble with that approach is that we aren't adding arrows to our quiver. It is wise to equip ourselves to deal with a wide variety of situations. As a coach, I try to help people find their alternative responses.

It starts with identifying where it is that we get triggered, and learning where we get stuck. When somebody says X, and our reaction is Y, how can we instead have reaction Z? In short, we can do so by being true to ourselves and allowing ourselves to be vulnerable enough to explore a different way. As we learn more about ourselves, we hone the skills that serve us well in the office, in the home and among friends.

> *You can change yourself quicker than you can change others.*

After coaching, businesspeople often say that they are thinking differently at home, or in the community, or at the Rotary Club. That's because when we add to our thinking, it doesn't just serve us in one place. Those lessons will invariably find an application somewhere else. We step into the same river. Wherever we go, we take these new skills with us.

If one approach doesn't work, then you will be able to try another. It's on your own back that you wear that quiver of arrows. You are the one deciding the right time to reach for a different arrow for the task at hand. You can change yourself quicker than you can change others. When you make a difference in yourself, you can then change your relationships and your results.

THE TURNING POINT

Each of us can think of times when we struggled and how those actually became times when we started on a newer, wiser path to success. It's almost as if we fade before we grow. Often, we can identify our turnaround as that point when someone showed us candor.

During my banking career, I reached a point where I wasn't sure how to attain the next level of growth I wanted. There was something to be done next, but I was worried that I might not be up to it. I might not be the one who could take it to the next level. That fear made me step out of the world of possibility.

That's when I engaged a coach. I needed someone who would help me to think things through and get my self-generated barriers out of the way so that I could think more broadly and with more possibility; someone who had no agenda with the company and with whom I could interact more as a peer; someone who could look at things anew with me. That's what coaching is all about, a comfortable relationship in which I could explore ideas for experimenting and innovating. I could be true to myself, with no one judging.

I was a coaching client when I realized that the assistance I was receiving was the same kind of assistance I had been offering to a lot of other people. I was asking questions. I was giving support. I was helping people to stretch their potential by what I asked them. I had been doing that all along for others. I found that I loved both being coached and coaching others.

Today, I am privileged to work daily with smart and successful business people who have a lifelong curiosity about how to improve relationships and results. They want to be even more effective. They are developing enterprises that are creating a lot of jobs, and they are doing good things in the community. I get to meet dairy farmers and manufacturers, work with scientists and C-suite executives. I have the pleasure of learning about their businesses and the passions of people who value success, who make our society thrive. My role is to help draw out of them a sense of clarity about the path they wish to pursue. My career is a joy.

> *I know that on the path to greater success, it is a good idea to reach out to others, in order to learn more about myself.*

I am a coach who knows what it is like to be a client, who has been one and who understands firsthand what it feels like to be in transition and uncertain of what lies ahead. I have seen how it has benefited me, and I can empathize with the range of feelings involved. I know that on the path to greater success, it is a good idea to reach out to others, in order to learn more about myself.

SOMEDAY IS HERE

Candor is the element that we often need to develop without delay in our organizations. Companies function far better when candor is endemic to the culture, and when the leaders are true to themselves and to their goals. Leaders attain greater heights when they eschew the spin, the judgmental critiquing, the blaming, and the traits that hinder progress. By forging better relationships, they accelerate the velocity of their success.

We all benefit by asking ourselves whether we are doing what we love. No job can be joy every moment, but a career should fulfill. A lot of people feel discontented because they have yet to figure out how to do what they love, or they haven't been honest with themselves about what it might take, or they think they will do that when they retire someday.

When is someday? I have known too many people who didn't make it to retirement, or who dreamed of doing something they're no longer able to do. Sometimes they waited too long before identifying their purpose and passion. Now is not too soon.

ABOUT THE AUTHOR:

Photo by Maguiresphoto.com

As a business coach and consultant for CEOs, entrepreneurs, nonprofit leaders, and boards of directors, Nancy K. Eberhardt has discovered how fostering an atmosphere of authentic conversation can translate into success. Clients feel comfortable opening up within her environment of mutual respect and new possibilities, quickly getting to the heart of what matters.

A former regional bank president, Eberhardt was responsible for $1 billion in customer relationships and a number of significant mergers. This experience as a successful business leader allows her to relate to her clients from a shared perspective. Her educational background is in industrial/organizational psychology and leadership coaching, and she teaches business communications to Executive MBA students. She posts frequent blogs on her *Uncommon Candor* website, and is a regular guest contributor on the Gazelles International Coaches blog.

Eberhardt's core commitment to service and her deep love of baseball have led her to positions with the boards of directors of a community bank, a social venture corporation, a stadium authority, the only national park for the performing arts, and major nonprofit agencies.

Most leaders have great ideas and high expectations for their organizations. They know where they stand financially and may know where they want to lead their team. However, they find that they are not moving at the speed they once experienced or had hoped to see.

Eberhardt brings to her clients an understanding of an executive's point of view, because she has been there. She knows what it takes to build success from the inside out and helps clients guide their teams to execute flawlessly by sharing the same vision and bringing it to fruition. Then they can begin to lead a culture that not only fosters growth and accomplishment but also increases the value of the organization.

Her clients at Pathwise Partners invest significant time, effort and energy into making changes in their organizations. But they have found that those efforts alone do not always produce the results that they want. They may feel as if they are working harder than ever, yet the needle isn't moving as it should.

What matters next? What does the future hold? How do you get there? Those are the questions that Eberhardt, working with clients as their committed partner, helps to answer. Together, they assess not just what they are doing now but how to develop the smartest strategy for the short and long term, a clear path to building an efficient and results-oriented organization, in which candor is the operating principle and all receive the honor they deserve.

Printed in the USA
CPSIA information can be obtained
at www.ICGtesting.com
JSHW012054140824
68134JS00035B/3425